CONTENT

INTRODUCTION

Our Manual of Modern Small Plywood Boat Construction Techniques covers the construction of stitch and tape boats up to 16 feet (4.9m) or so. This manual continues the description of plywood boats above this length. Many of the chapters on the use of epoxies in boat construction in the Small Plywood Manual are also relevant to large plywood boats but at around 20 feet (6.1m), the way I design the construction of plywood boats, often changes.

Why does it change? Stitch and tape construction uses pre-shaped plywood hull panels/planks which are stitched along their mating edges. These 'chine' seams are then finished in glass tape and epoxy. The plywood frames and bulkheads are often "dropped" into the hull and epoxy filleted to the inside of the hull panels – there is therefore no formal wood framework as such, which is often the advantage of stitch and tape.

However, with bigger boats, the hull panels are correspondingly larger and much heavier, with thicker plywood being used. Trying to get these panels into their correct place can

Above— an example of a simple stitch and tape framework construction, in this case a Selway Fisher Ptarmigan 17 by Mr. P. Phillips showing the hull panels epoxied together and the plywood frames/bulkheads inserted epoxy filleted to the hull panels.

3

be quite a struggle, even with several helping hands. Without a supporting reference framework, it is difficult to have any reference line or surface and therefore, it is more difficult on bigger boats to achieve the true and proper shape for the hull.

Also, the larger the boat, the bigger the epoxy joins – in a small dinghy you may use just one piece of 2" or 3" (50mm or 75mm) wide tape in epoxy resin. As you go up to a dayboat, the chine joins between the panels may have an epoxy fillet overlaid with one or two pieces of 3" (75mm) glass tape. Above 20 feet (6.1m) you will start to use much greater quantities of epoxy with chine seams consisting of maybe 3 layers of tape in different widths over a large epoxy fillet plus the same on the outside. The point at which the efficiency in using epoxy, of low construction time and low construction skills, starts to dwindle, I find, at around 20' (6.1m). At this point, more conventional plywood construction starts to become the better way to go, whilst at the same time, using epoxy fillets elsewhere in the construction, where they are most beneficial.

Having a framework to work too, on bigger boats, is also a great help – if the framework is rigid and accurately set up, you are starting on the correct course to finishing a well found boat. The stresses imposed by ballast keels, inboard engines and stern gear, larger centreplates and bigger masts etc., are substantially more than on a small boat and a framework to distribute these stresses is often needed anyway. So, if some sort of frame work or 'space frame' is required to do the job of stress distribution in a larger boat, you might just as well use it to get the shape of the boat correct and help in the planking process.

Boats over 20' (6.1m) also tend to have

accommodation – dinettes, chart areas, galleys, bunks etc – all of which need subdivision. In a good design, the accommodation requirements would be incorporated into the frame work at the same time. If the bulkheads and girders also form divisions and bunk/cockpit fronts, then none of the framework becomes redundant after the hull is built.

Above—a Selway Fisher CR25 by Mr. Sam Watts under construction showing a modern ply on frame set-up with plywood frames and girders slotted together and chine and gunwale stringers.

So, in summary, what does, or can, a framework do?

- It provides a reference structure for the boat.
- It distributes stresses around the hull.
- It can be used to help subdivide the interior into the accommodation required.
- It provides a frame system onto which the hull skin is attached and is also an aid to shaping the hull panels.

You will find that this manual approaches Ply on Frame Construction by first looking at the different types of frameworks that we might choose and how they differ from each other. We will look at the tools you might need to use and the kind of workshop facilities that would be ideal to have, along with the choice of design you may go for.

We will also look at the different wood joins which are relevant and the type of wood and glues you might use. Marking and setting out will be covered next, followed by setting up the framework accurately with a look at the type of chine joins you might go for before we discuss the planking process.

Finally, we will look at simple wood skegs and deadwood, decks, superstructures and finishing the hull. Machinery installation, ballast keels, rudders, electrics and plumbing are covered in the Selway Fisher Manual of Fit-Out for yachts.

I hope you find the manual useful.

Paul Fisher BSc. MRINA
2009

Below—a Selway Fisher CR25 by Mr. Sam Watts finished and ready for the water.

Chapter 1

FRAMEWORKS
TRADITIONAL & MODERN FRAMEWORKS FOR PLYWOOD CONSTRUCTION

1.1 Traditional Frameworks for Ply Over Frame Construction

By 'Traditional Frameworks', I mean the type of frameworks used before the advent of marine epoxies and CAD software on modern PC's. This type of framework consists of a lot of small pieces of wood carefully joined together to make up a rigid framework.

Let me illustrate this and at the same time 'name' the typical components/parts of a framework.

The frames themselves (the athwartship – sideways) part of the framework are often made from timber with halved or ply gusseted joins. Sometimes the timber frame

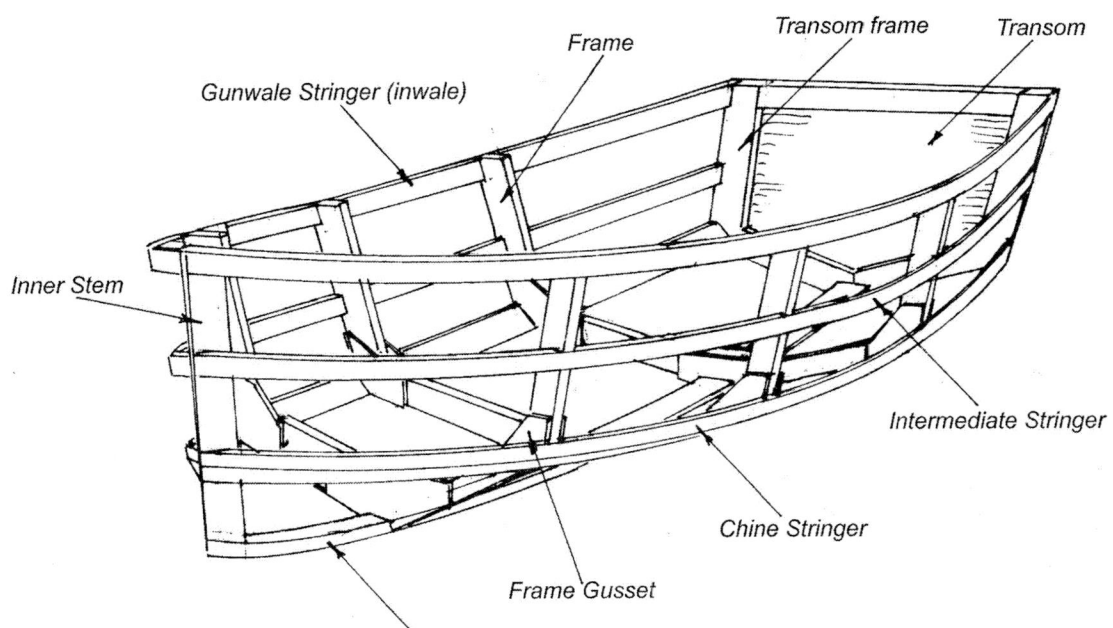

Fig 1. A traditional framework for ply over frame construction.

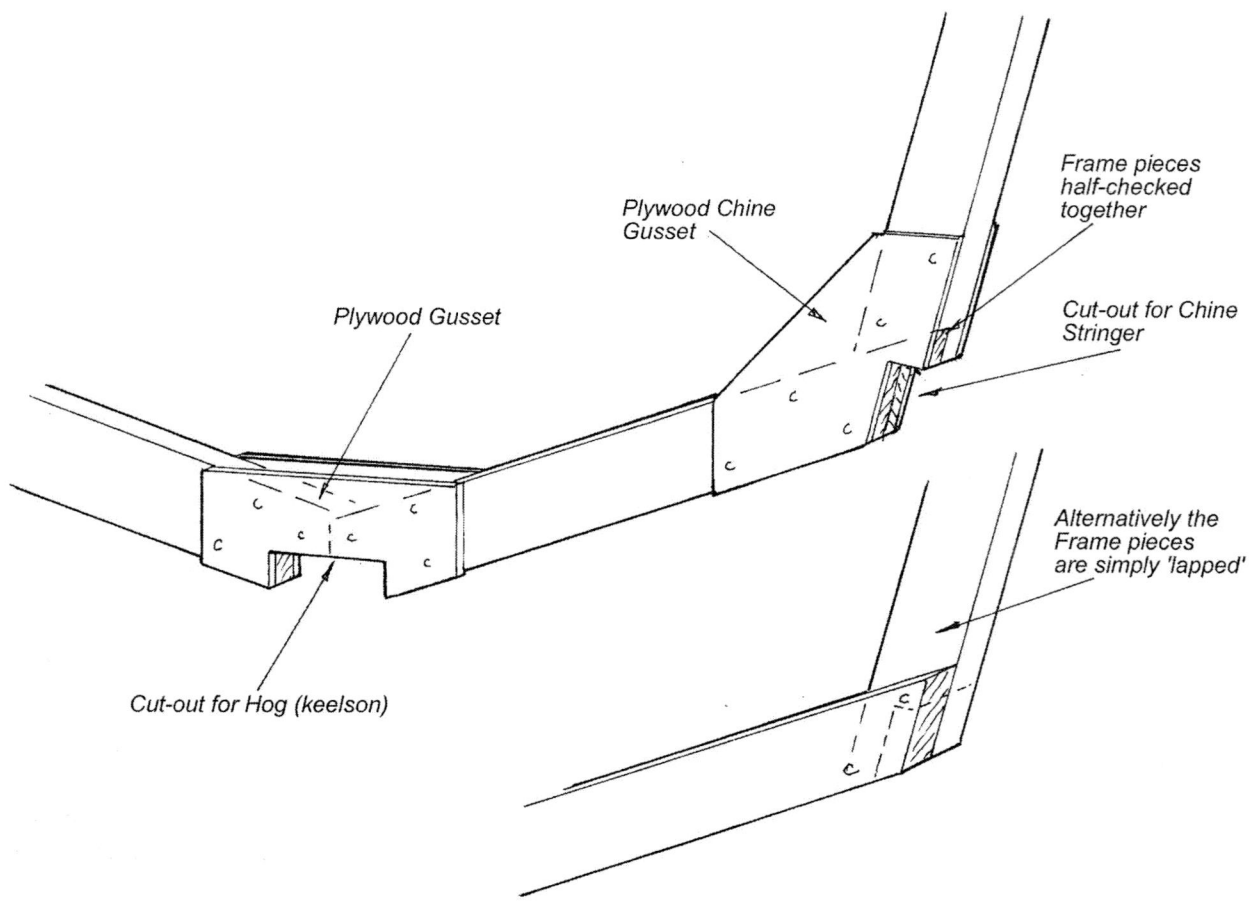

Plywood Chine
Gusset

Frame pieces
half-checked
together

Plywood Gusset

Cut-out for Chine
Stringer

Alternatively the
Frame pieces
are simply 'lapped'

Cut-out for Hog (keelson)

Fig 2. Timber frames made up with gusseted joins and with more simple 'lapped' joins.

pieces are simply 'lapped' without gussets (Figure 2). Gusseted joins are very strong especially if the timber frame pieces are also half-checked together (see Chapter 3 for half-checked joins). Lapped joins were often used in fairly crude plywood workboats and were fine if the timber used for the frame pieces was fairly wide allowing a good gluing area between the adjacent pieces.

To 'balance' the construction of the individual frame, a gusset is usually applied on both sides of the frame unless one side is against a plywood bulkhead or frame, in which case, it is often acceptable to use the plywood frame/bulkhead as a large gusset and strength member without the need for a

further gusset on the side of the timber frame not attached to the plywood frame/bulkhead.

These frames were often erected upside down, onto a building floor along with the stem and transom. The centreline structure was taken care of with an inner keelson or hog which was secured into slots cut in the frames to accept it and the same was done for the chines and gunwales with chine and gunwale stringers. In the early days of plywood construction, the stem (and sometimes, the keelson/hog) were rabbeted in the traditional way to accept the plywood planking (Figure 3).

Some traditional frameworks combined the solid wood framing with plywood partitioning in the form of bulkheads but few brought in fore and aft plywood dividers at this stage – fore and aft bulkheads were often fitted after the hull had been planked and of course, turned over.

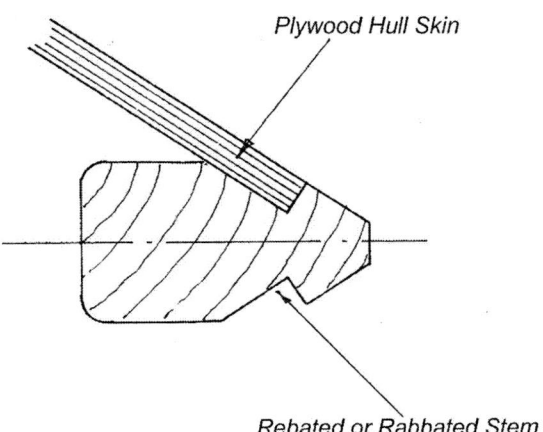

Fig 3. A traditional 'rabbeted' stem piece.

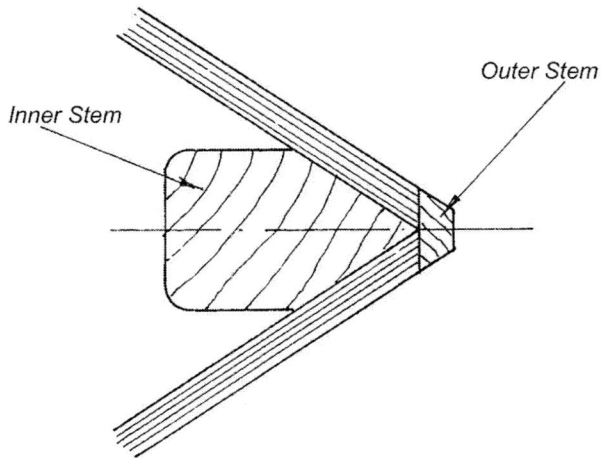

Fig 4. A modern 'batten' stem with separate inner and outer parts allowing easier fitting of the plywood planking—the inner stem is simply 'chamfered' to accept the planking rather than being rabbated.

With the advent of better glues and with an increase in home construction calling for fewer traditional boatbuilding skills, the stem was separated into 2 parts – inner and outer, with the outer stem added later to cover the end grain of the plywood skin.

As you can see, traditional framework construction for plywood boats still required a fair amount of woodworking skill both in terms of wood joinery and in terms of accurate setting up.

Because of the many individual components, this type of framework tends to be heavier than the more modern type of framework which depends more on plywood alone.

In the 1990's yacht design and CAD software became available for use on home computers. This allowed the designer to accurately produce the shape of plywood components on the computer screen and allowed a fresh look at frameworks with a

view to cutting out as many components as possible, making construction easier, quicker and cheaper.

Effectively, making a traditional framework with all it's many components, meant that you were "fairing" the hull, on the job, so to speak. Frames could be planed back or "packed out" to fair the hull surface ready to accept the planking. There was no great problem in doing this, but modern computer software has allowed the designer to fair the hull and produce millimetre accurate frame shapes before construction starts.

1.2 Modern Frameworks for Ply Over Frame Construction

Good boat design tries to avoid "redundancy" in the construction – you don't want a particular component to do a job and then be left in the boat serving no other purpose once that first job is fulfilled. The obvious way to achieve this, is to make frameworks form partitions for the interior layout or, form strength members to transmit stresses and take the loads that the hull has to take from rigging, rudders, keels, engines etc.

Again, in our attempt to reduce the number of individual pieces of wood used in a framework, where it is sensible to do so, we can replace wood filleting and cleats with epoxy fillets. But, as mentioned previously, we should only take this as far as it is

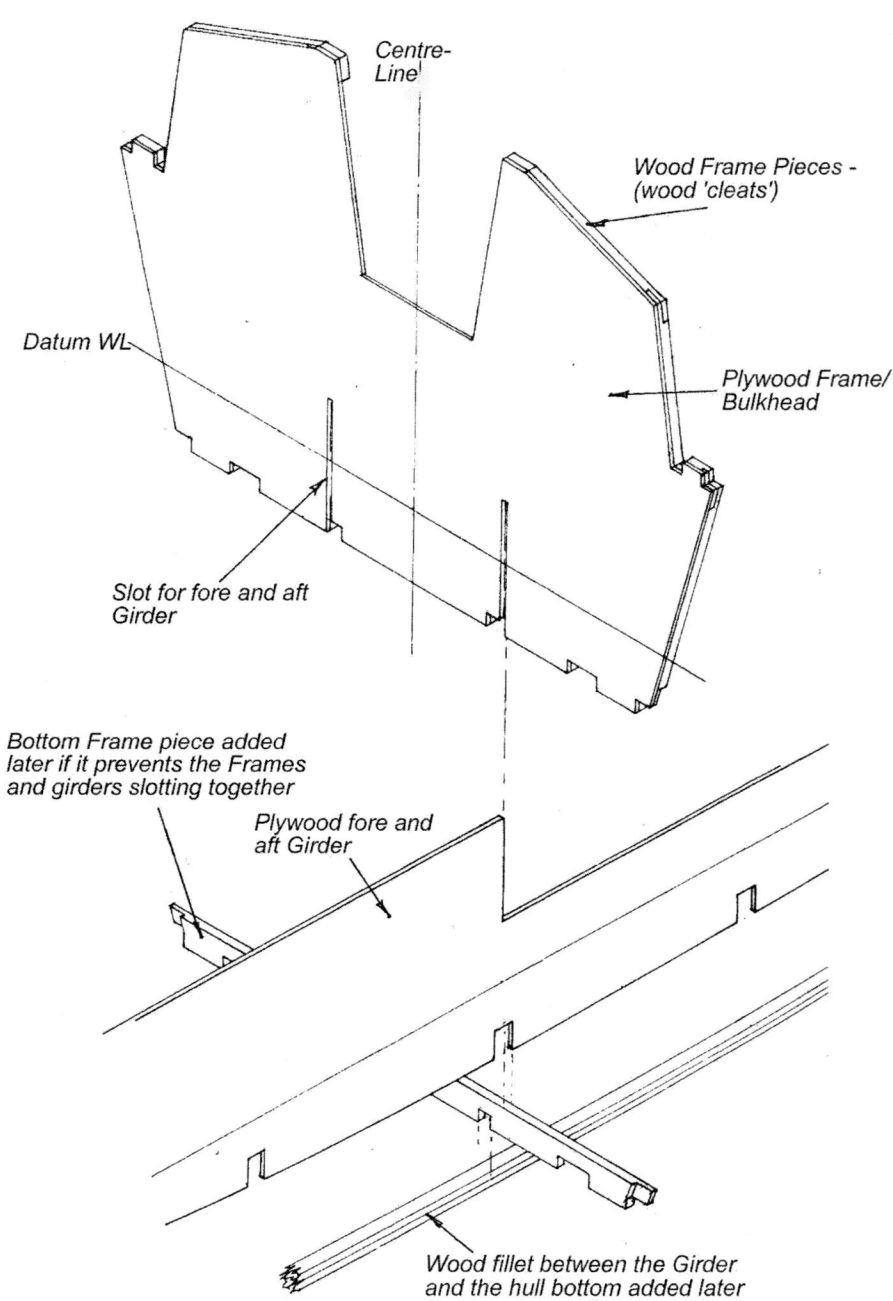

Fig 5. A modern 'egg-box' framework with slotted frames/bulkheads and fore and aft girders.

economical and practical to do so – large boats require large fillets, requiring large amounts of what is, very expensive epoxy resin (in racing boats of course, you may also use epoxy rather than wood fillets to keep weight down, but that is not the type of boat covered by this manual).

Traditional frameworks tended to have fore and aft ply dividers added at a later stage. So bunk and cockpit fronts would have there shapes taken from the hull itself after it had been turned over. Adding longitudinal plywood sub dividers this way does give you the freedom to move these "fronts" or bulkheads where you want, but why not see if you can combine them and have a cockpit front that becomes a bunk front or galley front as it goes forward past the main bulkhead into the boat – and we can have a stem girder which defines the shape of the bow and goes aft, either splitting into side girders for the bunk fronts or becoming the centreboard case (if we have one).

If we make these components continuous fore and aft as far as possible, we end up with a fore and aft strength member as well as a sub divider for the accommodation – and if

Above—a Selway Fisher 22' Black Swan by Uri Fischer with plywood frames/bulkheads and girders slotted together (kit by Jordan Boats).

we lock these fore and aft plywood girders with the athwartships/transverse plywood frames and bulkheads, we will end up with a structure, strong and stiff in all directions and which is already helping us with the fit-out of the interior.

Locking the athwartships/transverse frames with the fore and aft girders is a simple matter of cutting matching slots in each, so that the ply components slide together in an "egg-box" fashion (Figure 5).

If each of these components have the Datum Water Line and, where possible, the centreline, marked on them, then setting the framework up so that it is all square and level, is much easier.

1.3 Epoxy Fillets vs Wood Fillets for Joining Ply Components

Whether or not you use epoxy or wood fillets to join the ply bulkheads and girders together, depends on a number of factors.

First, a wood fillet, assuming that the fillet has been machined square, will help provide you with a good square framework where the angle between the fore and aft girders and the transverse frames/bulkheads are 90 degrees – be cautious here, as a wood fillet applied with more glue on one surface than the other can pull a framework out of 'true' (Figure 6) – and I have seen boat frameworks where this has happened even though the fillets were definitely machined square! So always check and do not assume that a square cut fillet will give you a square framework – but it will go a long way to help!

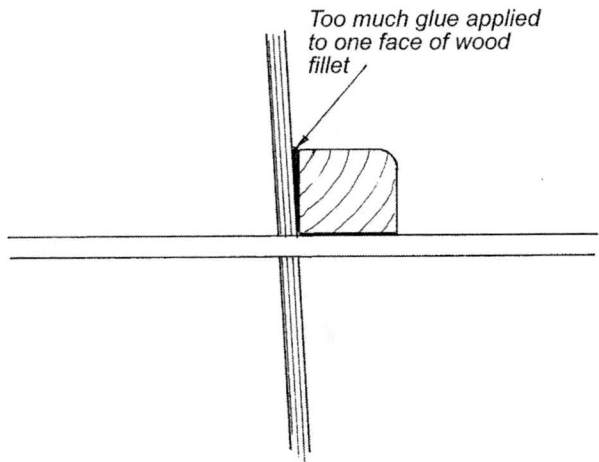

Fig 6. Framework taken out of 'true' by a badly fitted wood/glue fillet.

Having a wood fillet on both sides of a join helps this situation but may be going "over the top" strength-wise (Figure 7).

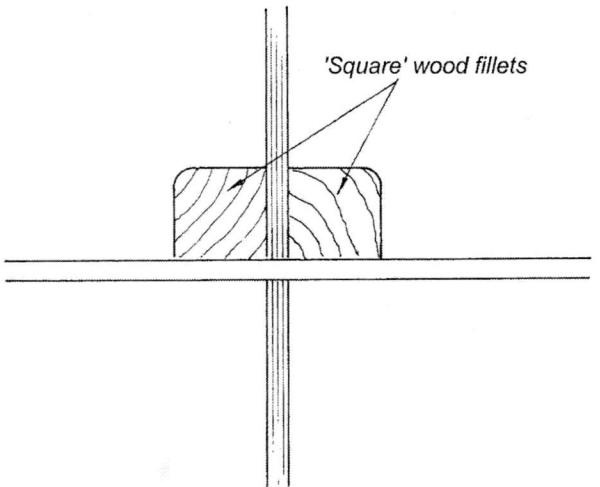

Fig 7. A double wood fillet join.

The reverse of this, is that with a structure where the plywood components are joined with epoxy fillets, you must make sure that the components are 'square' to each other before applying the epoxy fillet – once the fillets have cured, you cannot readjust the join.

Second, I like to put a structure together "dry" to start with – ie. without glue and using wood fillets allows you to do this easier and more accurately than just slotting the components together.

Third, as we have already mentioned, there are the costs to take into account – once your boat goes over 25-28' (7.6 – 8.5m) the epoxy quantites are quite big and become expensive.

If you do use epoxy fillets what size do they need to be? It depends on the size of boat and which components the epoxy is fixing together – ie. is it a simple join between two partitions or is it an area under more stress, near a mast support frame or the centreboard? For joins which are not under any great stress the general rule is that the radius of the fillet is 3 to 4 times the maximum thickness of plywood being joined. So if you are bonding 3/8" (9mm) thick plywood then the radius of the fillet would be just over 1 1/8" (27mm) and usually no larger than 1 1/2" (38mm).

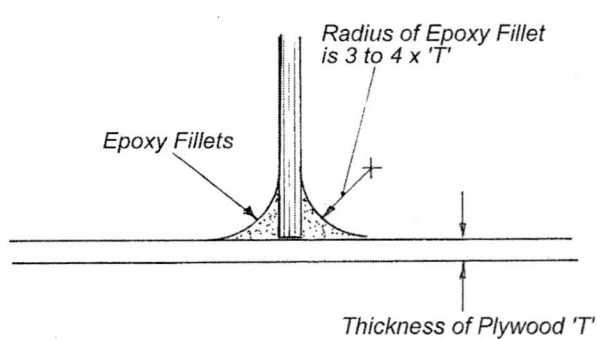

Fig 8. A simple epoxy filleted join.

Where the angle between the plywood in the join is obtuse (over 90 degrees) and a fillet based on radius would be impractical, it is better to use a fillet defined by it's thickness at it's mid-point. This would normally be at least 1.5 times the thickness of plywood being joined together (Figure 9).

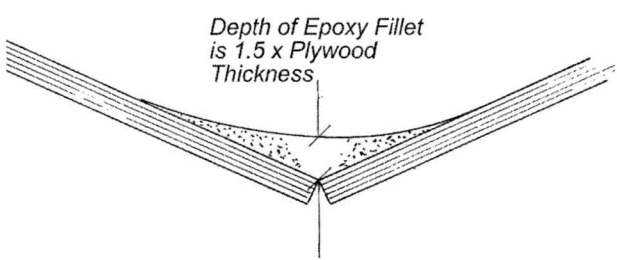

Fig 9. Size of epoxy fillet for an 'obtuse' join.

For joins which are under stress from the forces imposed by rigging, near rudders etc, I use a fillet combining thickened epoxy and woven glass tape. Here (Figure 10) is an example taken from the Selway Fisher 14' Heron Pocket Cruiser design in the centreline/hog area.

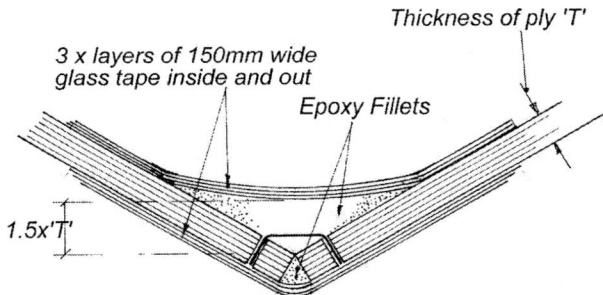

Fig 10. Typical combined glass and epoxy fillet.

Getting a good finish on epoxy fillets is not difficult. After a little practice, good, smooth, clean fillets can be achieved but there are one or two points which will make this process easier. First, do not try to over thicken the fillet in order to gain more filleting material. This simply starves the joint of resin making it weaker and rougher. Secondly, have a range of different sizes of spatula ready with radiused ends (you can either buy them or make them up from scrap ply/plastic).

Next, apply masking tape to the ply either side of the joint before you apply the epoxy. Although this may sound like extra expense and effort, the result is well worth it and if you have ever looked at professionally built boats and wondered how they achieved such smooth, straight and uniform fillets, taping the seam either side is how they do it. The tape should be removed before the epoxy cures and I do this carefully by pealing it back on itself straight after I have finished applying the epoxy fillet. Put the tape on before you prime the seam (Figure 11).

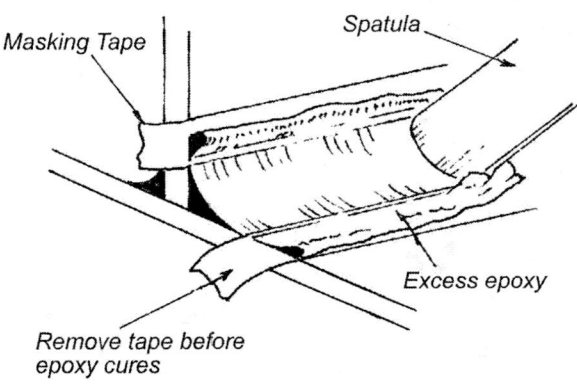

Fig 11. Getting a smart epoxy joint.

Two other things you can do. Use a chisel to carefully scrape off any excess epoxy (especially if you have not used tape) but without digging the chisel into the wood!, and go over the fillet if it appears rough whilst it cures, with a rounded knife to smooth down bumps.

1.4 Notes on Using Epoxies for Bonding Wood Components

To keep costs down, I tend to use Marine adhesives (Balcotan, Cascamite, Aerolite 306 etc) for most gluing jobs. Using conventional glues for gunwales, thwarts, knees etc is perfectly alright but you may wish to take advantage of the high strength and gap filling properties of epoxies for bonding and gluing items which are subjected to high stress. Mast steps, centreboard/daggerboard cases, engine beds, scarf or butt joints in hull panels and stringers are candidates for this type of treatment.

The process is quite simple. First, dry fit the components together, make sure they fit and devise a way of clamping them whilst the epoxy cures. Next, prime all surfaces with epoxy resin and then apply thickened resin as the glue. The resin is simply thickened with a small amount of Microfibres until a ''Ketchup'' consistancy is achieved which sags and will not hold a shape when it is moved around in the mixing pot.

Bring the components together and clamp lightly until the mixture squeezes out. The epoxy has the advantage over other adhesives in that it will fill gaps in construction and does not need high clamping forces. If you are bonding a very porous wood such as balsa, cedar or spruce, pre coat the surfaces and let them cure before applying the priming coat and thickened resin. Likewise, if you are bonding the end grain of wood and the surface appears dry and flat, then this will need pre coating.

If you have large gaps in the joint, then the resin should be thicker. Any clamping system can be employed which produces even pressure over the whole surface and I often use rope, string and rubber cut from old inner tubes. The components tend to slip over each other more easily with the epoxy than they may do with ordinary adhesives and I therefore find on thin ply, that it is a good idea to use 1 or 2 staples to prevent this. On larger components, even though they are not needed for strength, screws which have been tried at the dry fit stage are also very helpful to keep the components in their correct position.

For components like centreboard case logs, it is a good idea to make a gap for the epoxy to sit in (Figure 12). This ensures a strong joint through and through with no possibility of epoxy starvation. Therefore the faces of the logs should be slightly bevelled and the subsequent gap produced against the case side primed and filled with thickened epoxy.

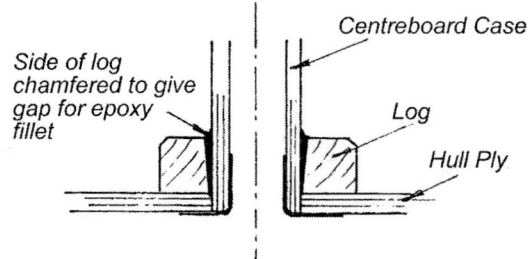

Fig 12. Gap formed for epoxy fillet.

1.5 The Choice of Design

This leads to the choice of plywood design you might make for your project – although this manual is primarily about the more modern method of ply on frame construction, there is much in it to help those who are working to the plans of an older design.

There is every possibility, if you want to save time, money and weight, to convert an older plywood design to more modern methods of construction. However, this may have to be done by a designer but, if areas like cockpit and bunk/seat fronts are in line with each other, or can be moved so that they do correspond in the line they take, then you will be able to go for the "egg-box" type of construction of modern plywood designs.

At the very least, it is usually possible to change the individual wood stem to a ply central girder which will make setting up much easier. I will not go into this in great depth here as it is really material for a completely separate book but, you may find enough information and ideas on how to do this from the illustrations and material in this manual.

Selway Fisher have undertaken this sort of exercise and have a good experience of the pitfalls that can occur and we are happy for you to consult us on making these types of changes to older plywood designs.

Two views of two different Selway Fisher Black Swans—the upper one in Saudi Arabia and the lower one in Germany— both showing the egg-box type plywood framing used in the plywood version of this design.

Above and Left—a Selway Fisher Martlet 30 yacht under construction by Phillip Ruewell— the plywood frames with their edge cleats have been erected onto a strongback. In the left picture you can just see the forward plywood girder which also forms the inner stem shape.

Left is another picture of Sam Watt's Selway Fisher CR25 showing the plywood framing with the chine stringers and inwale fitted along with the flat bottom and garboard planks.

Right is Nick Croome's Selway Fisher 25'5" Shang-hai Cruising Junk—in this case assembled upright— the plywood fore and aft girder and flat bottom panel form a 'T' girder onto which the frames are slotted—building this way means that much of the interior fit-out can be easily done before the hull is planked.

Chapter 2

THE WORK AREA
TOOLS AND BASIC MEASURING SKILLS REQUIRED

2.1 General Comments

Our Manual of Small Plywood Boat Construction Techniques goes into the construction of simple temporary workshops, which can be scaled up for bigger boats, in detail. As far as space and building environment is concerned, remember that this is not going to be a small project in terms of time. In embarking on the construction of a boat over 24' (7.3m) or so in length, you are starting something which will involve at least several 1000 hours in the construction and which is going to cost you a lot of money. This is not a simple canoe or dinghy project and because of the length of time it takes to build it, the boat you are building may sit for sometime, especially during winter months or times when you have other priorities, unattended. So a simple basic shelter may not be enough.

You will also have to store relatively large amounts of expensive materials – maybe 30 or 40 sheets of plywood and many lengths of timber plus all the epoxies etc. These are all high investment items and must not be allowed to deteriorate during construction.

The investment in tools goes up for a larger project too. You will find that machines such as planner/thicknessers, band saws, circular saws and pillar drills have now come down in cost relative to what they were a few years ago. These machines are worth having as they can cut down preparation time dramatically. They will also need space for safe and efficient use.

So what I am saying is, in choosing where you are going to build the boat, you may have to be quite ambitious. A good, well heated and well lit barn with a concrete floor and plenty of power points would be ideal. Having said that, I have worked in temporary thrown up work shops. However, in this type of environment you to need to plan carefully when you do certain parts of the project such as the main epoxy work which requires higher temperatures and a dry atmosphere.

It all comes down to giving yourself the best chance of successfully finishing the project. You do not want to end up with a half finished hull that becomes a burden or a giant flower pot in the garden!

2.2 The Size of the Workshop

I have worked in very tight work areas where I have had to push the framework and hull from side to side in order to work on each side, separately. This is a far from ideal situation and not to be recommended, especially in the freezing conditions I was working in!

I like to have a workshop with at least 4' (1.2m) clear at each end of the boat and at least half the beam of the boat clear to each side (Figure 13). Unfortunately, it is often rare to be able to work in this amount of space – but keep this kind of space in mind if you are making your own workshop. The spaces required for materials, machinery and workbench are in addition to the workspace for the boat.

For the building floor, I have worked straight off mud, which I have previously ensured was flat, but if you are going to loft or draw down a large boat and especially if you want to make sure that you have a good flat level working platform, then this can be made out

of a simple timber framework covered with ¾" (18mm) chipboard. The framework can then be 2"x 4" (50x100mm) Fir/Deal or larger, with half checked or butted and filleted joins (Figure 14).

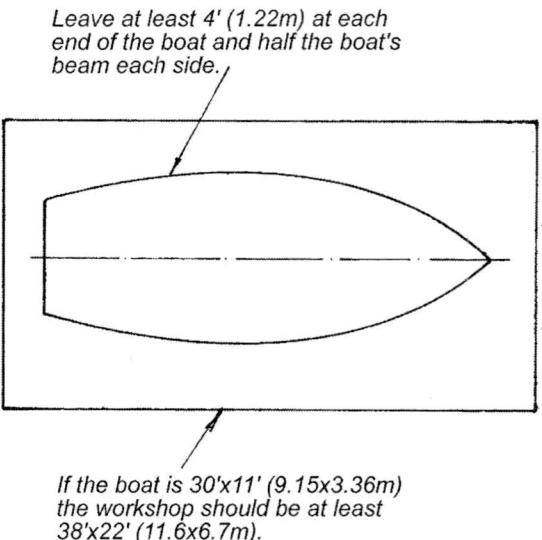

Leave at least 4' (1.22m) at each end of the boat and half the boat's beam each side.

If the boat is 30'x11' (9.15x3.36m) the workshop should be at least 38'x22' (11.6x6.7m).

Fig 13. The workshop space (for the boat only).

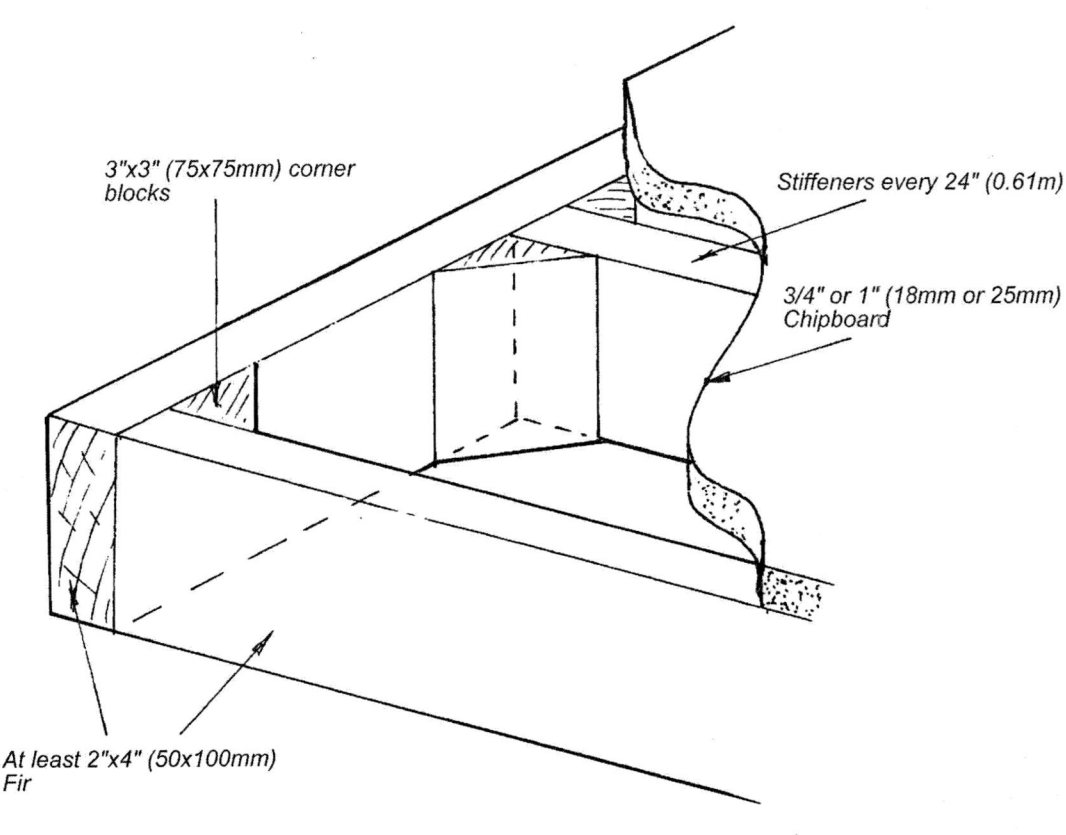

3"x3" (75x75mm) corner
blocks

Stiffeners every 24" (0.61m)

3/4" or 1" (18mm or 25mm)
Chipboard

At least 2"x4" (50x100mm)
Fir

Fig 14. A simple workshop floor.

2.3 The Tools You Will Need

This is just a suggested list for what I consider to be the minimum tool kit required to construct a large plywood boat.

For marking out:

- A 4' and 6' (1.2m and 1.8m) straight edge (or a good straight piece of timber).
- A 10' (3m) tape measure (or longer if possible).
- Several good sharp pencils (I keep loosing them!).
- A large carpenter's square.
- A plumb line (can be a large nut or bolt attached to a piece of string).
A short and long carpenter's spirit level.

For cutting out and shaping:

- A domestic single or multi-speed speed jig saw of good quality – with screw driver capability.
- A small block plane.
- A Jack plane.
- A rebate plane.
- A honing stone (for sharpening your blades).
- 6, 9, 12, 18 and 24mm chisels.
- A tenon saw – high quality.
- A rip saw.
- A 10 oz. (or heavier if you prefer) hammer.
- A nail punch.
- A screw driver set.
- 2 electric drills – powerful and of good quality – 1 at least with a chuck that can handle up to 9mm bits.
- A hand drill with drill bits up to 9mm in dia.
- A set of good quality flat bits.
- A set of plug cutters.

- A Bradawl.
- A range of G cramps from 4" and up – as many as you can get (12 minimum) and a selection of German cramps plus at least 1 pair of sash cramps.
- 2 Black & Decker type Workmate folding workbenches – heavy duty.
- A portable planer.
- A router.
- A variety of sanding machines – good quality – I find a good palm sander very useful.
A set of thread cutting dies (if you are required to fit bolts).

Consumable Items etc

These are items other than tools that you will need during the construction.

- Large/small yogurt type pots - for glue/resin mixing.
- Mixing sticks - like large lollipop sticks.
- Barrier cream - to protect your hands.
- Acetone - for cleaning items coated in resin.
- Masking tape - for holding some items together whilst gluing and for masking off areas that you do not want covered in glue/resin.
String/rope for use as tourniquets and Spanish windlasses to hold panels in place during the stitching process.

2.4 Basic Marking Out

Some designs come with frame, bulkhead, transom and stem shapes full-size on large pieces of paper – DO NOT rely on these, unless they come on a Polyester or Mylar film (which is expensive) and even then, check and check again.

On every boat I have helped build which has full-size templates we have ended up having to make adjustments by referring to the original lines, offsets or measurements given on the plans – or by making adjustments on the framework itself. Paper plans distort and so always check. Care taken at this point will pay dividends later.

The modern alternative is to use CAD files either to get the frames etc plotted onto a good grade of film or paper or to give to a company with CNC facilities who can take the files (usually dxf or dwg) and rout or laser cut the shapes out for you. Not every designer is happy to provide CAD files, either because they cannot, or because of the fear that with the electronic data out of their control, they have no idea exactly how many boats are being built from their design. Dxf files are easily e-mailed which makes security difficult. At Selway Fisher Design we are happy to issue CAD files if we trust who we are dealing with.

Forgetting the CAD/CNC path at the moment, and going back to good old fashioned pencil and ruler methods for marking out, it is for the reasons that can be inherent in many full-size paper patterns that I prefer to use measurements and draw out the main components for the framework by hand directly onto the ply sheets.

In drawing out the frame/ bulkhead and transom shapes for a multi-chine plywood boat, there will be 2 main reference lines. The first is the centreline – this is the vertical line (or plane) which runs fore and aft down the centre of the boat. The second is usually some base or Datum line, which is horizontal and represents a plane running in the transverse direction (Figure 15).

Fig 15. The two axis/planes from which measurements are taken.

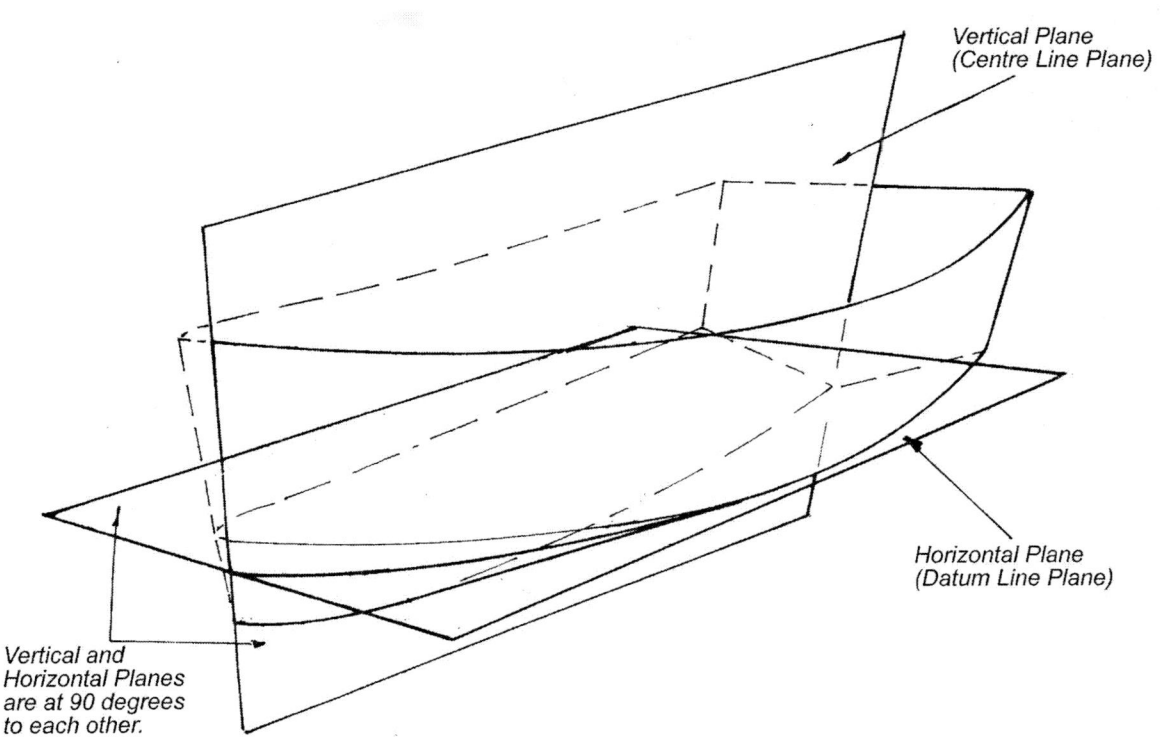

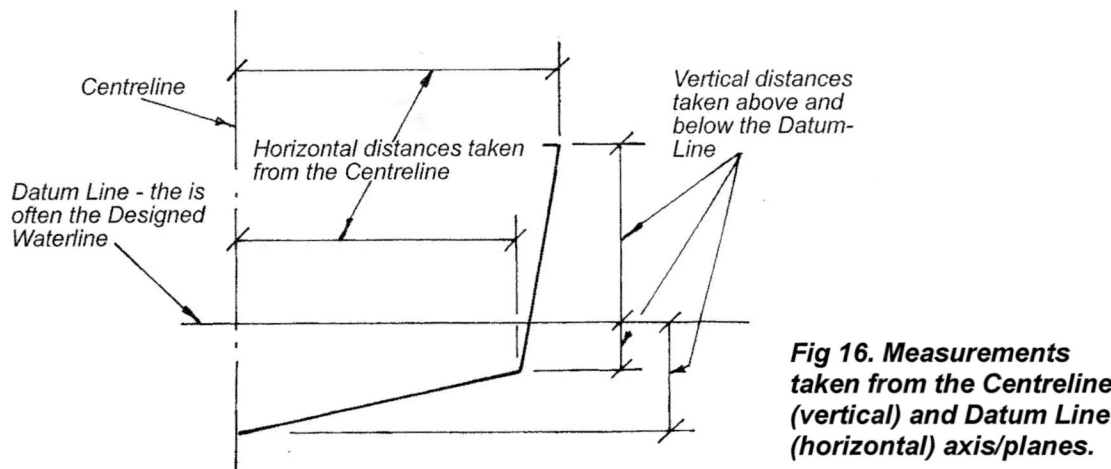

Fig 16. Measurements taken from the Centreline (vertical) and Datum Line (horizontal) axis/planes.

All horizontal distances to chine points, cut outs in the bulkheads etc are taken from the centreline and all heights are marked from the Datum/Base line – either above it, or below it (Figure 16).

If these 2 reference lines are marked accurately onto each plywood component, then you will be able to mark each component out accurately and set it up accurately too.

These 2 reference lines are obviously at 90 degrees to each other and so, we have to have an accurate way of setting up 2 lines, the centreline and datum/base line, at 90 degrees (right angles) to each other. For small components, it is perfectly acceptable to use a 'square' or a draftsman's 'set square'. But these are not usually very big and using them to set up the 90 degrees between the 2 reference lines on a large component becomes inaccurate. The best and easiest way to set up a right angle accurately is by using the arc or diagonal method.

This simply means using a compass (a pencil on a length of string) with it's centre at the intersection of the centreline and base/datum line, to tick off two points equidistant from the intersection (Figure 17). Move the centre

of your compass to each of these two points in turn and swing in two sets of arcs, on either side of the centreline and above and below the base/datum line, at each point. Where these arcs cross will be exactly perpendicular to the intersection between the centreline and the base/datum line and drawing a line through all three points will give you a line in the correct position and at 90 degrees to the centerline (Figure 17).

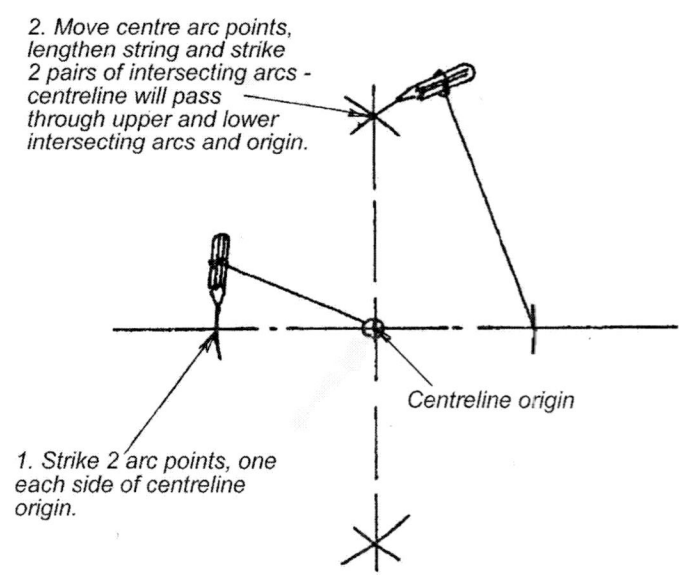

2. Move centre arc points, lengthen string and strike 2 pairs of intersecting arcs - centreline will pass through upper and lower intersecting arcs and origin.

Centreline origin

1. Strike 2 arc points, one each side of centreline origin.

Fig 17. Setting up 2 lines perpendicular (at 90 degrees) to each other.

22

If you have set up 2 lines at 90 degrees to each other, you can check the accuracy of the angle between them by using diagonal measurements as shown in Figure 18.

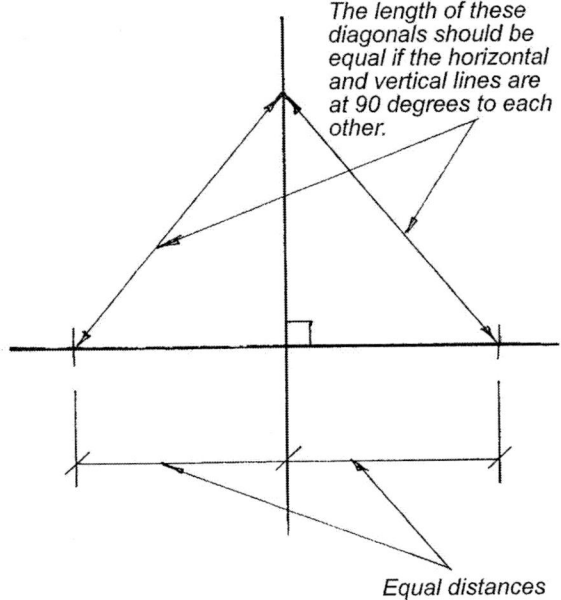

The length of these diagonals should be equal if the horizontal and vertical lines are at 90 degrees to each other.

Equal distances

Fig 18. Checking that 2 lines are perpendicular to each other.

A note of warning – it is very tempting to use one edge of a sheet of plywood as a reference line and to assume that the opposite edge is parallel to it and that the other edges are exactly at 90 degrees to the first edges. This is usually so, but do check – never take anything for granted!

Also, make sure that your reference lines are there to stay, can be easily seen and will not be rubbed off during the handling and cutting process.

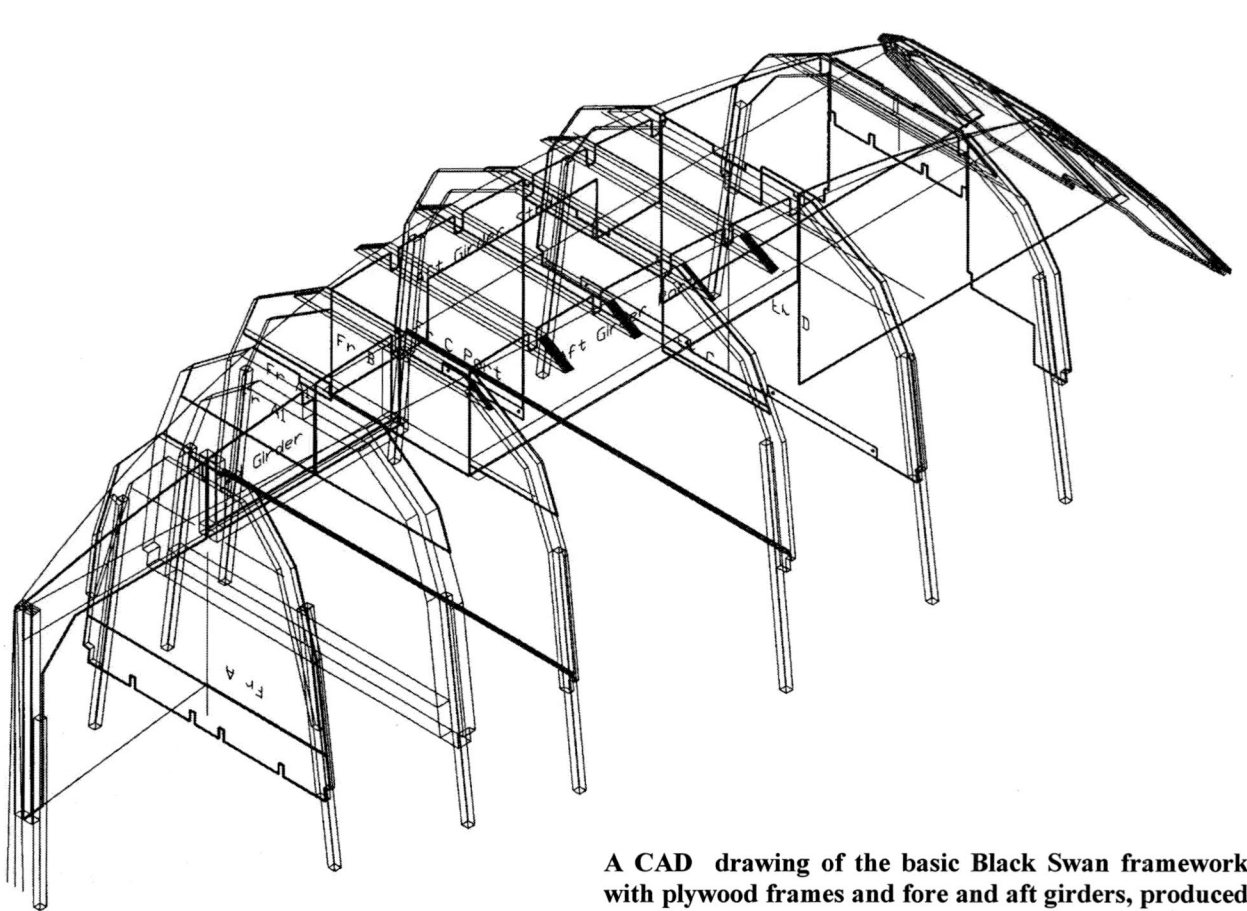

A CAD drawing of the basic Black Swan framework with plywood frames and fore and aft girders, produced by Jordan Boats as part of a plywood kit they made from Selway Fisher drawings—most of our plywood designs can be given the kit treatment by companies who specialize in this type of CAD work.

Chapter 3
COMMON WOOD JOINTS
USED IN LARGER PLYWOOD BOATS

3.1 Solid Wood Joints for Frame Construction

3.1.1 Typical Joints for Solid Wood

These are similar to those used in smaller plywood boat construction but there are usually more of them and on larger pieces of wood – so equip yourself with a solid bench to cut them on and use good quality tools to cut them with.

There are some simple joints that can be used and which will enhance the strength of the boat. These joints include those of the Halving family (the cross halving, tee halving, corner halving and dovetail halving) and also the finger/comb joints and bridle joints Figure 19).

Instead of going into a great discourse on actually how to mark and cut these joints out we have shown a series of sketches of these joints which are self explanatory. However, one or two points you should note if you are not familiar with simple joiner work are :-

1. Do equip yourself with a good square, a sharp pencil and a good tape measure and also use a good sharp backsaw (i.e. tenon saw) and a sharp chisel.

2. A large part of the strength of a joint is in the amount of gluing (faying) area that it has and therefore the type of joint chosen should depend to a certain extent on this.

3. Joints should be planed so that they do not weaken the structure. For instance if you have a stringer crossing a beam and both are

of similar depth (moulding), making a simple halving joint and removing half the depth of the beam, may badly effect the strength of the deck structure. Taking less out of the beam and more out of the stringer or using 2 angled halving joints may be better (Figure 20).

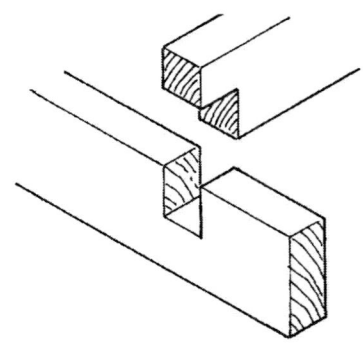

Fig 19b. TEE HALVING

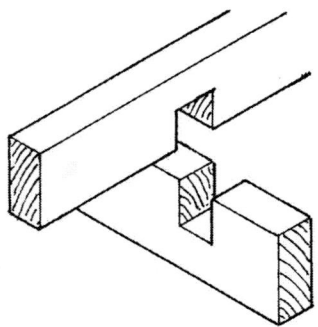

Fig 19a. CROSS HALVING

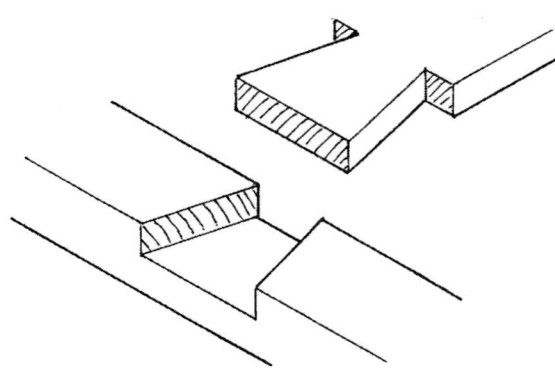

Fig 19d. DOVETAIL HALVING

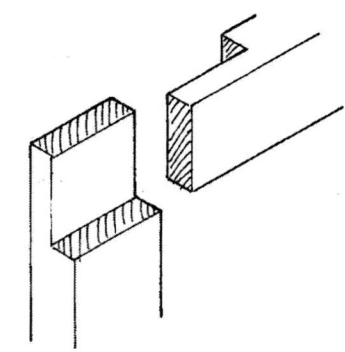

Fig 19c. CORNER HALVING

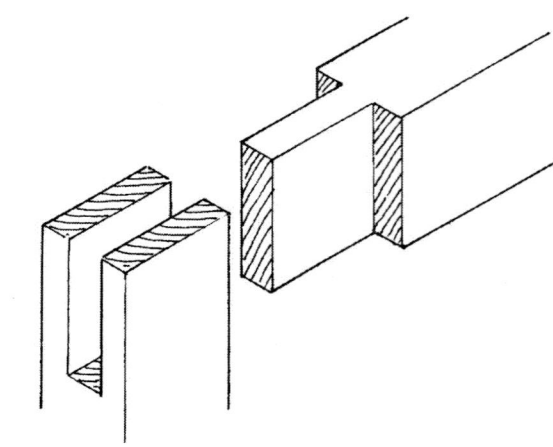

Fig 19f. BRIDLE

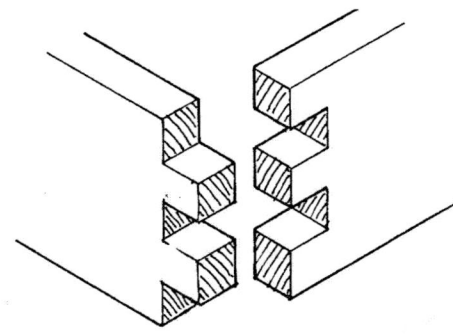

Fig 19e. FINGER/COMB

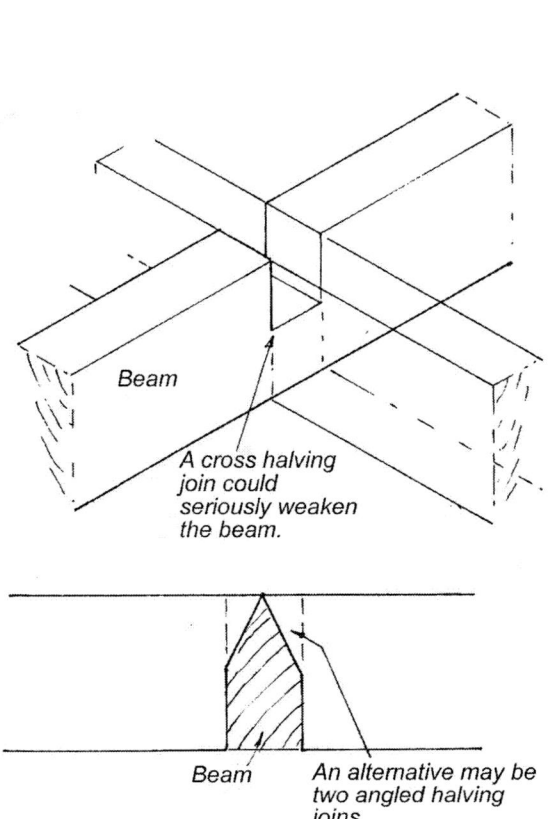

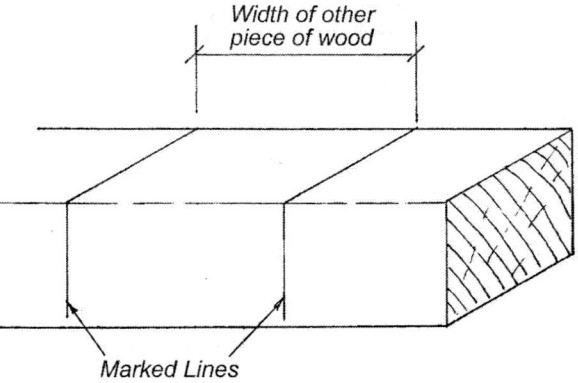

Fig 21.

Fig 20. Planning the joint for strength.

B. Note that half the material is removed from each of the pieces of wood therefore either by measuring down and drawing across or better still by using a marking gauge (if you can get used to using this tool) mark a line across either side which represents the bottom of the joint (Figure 22).

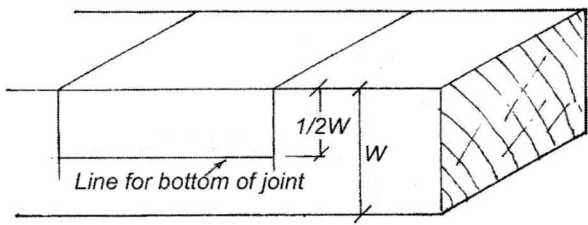

Fig 22.

Here is the sequence for making a good tee-halving joint and if you can do this joint, then you can do any of the other joints that are required.

A. Firstly mark the sides of the joint using the square across the wood and down each side (Figure 21) - a sharp pencil is essential.

C. It is a good idea to scribe these lines with a sharp knife cutting through the first few fibres of the wood Figure 23).

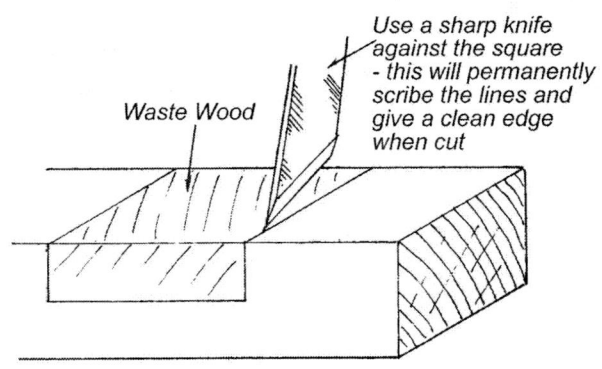

Fig 23.

D. Using your back saw (tenon saw) cut down to the bottom line carefully keeping the saw blade on the waste side of the line as shown. Do this for both lines and then cut two or three lines inside the joint (this will aid you when you come to chisel out the wood Figure 24).

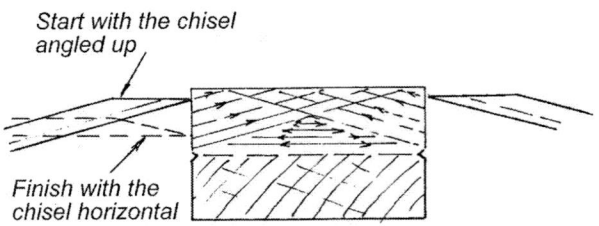

Start with the chisel angled up

Finish with the chisel horizontal

Fig 25.

the tee-halving joint this waste wood can be removed by two cuts of the backsaw making sure that you saw on the waste side of the line (Figure 26). By the way, it is a good idea to mark the waste wood that is to be removed, with diagonal lines, so that you remove the correct piece. It is very frustrating if you have got a long piece of wood with several pieces cut out of it to cut out the wrong piece and therefore ruin the work.

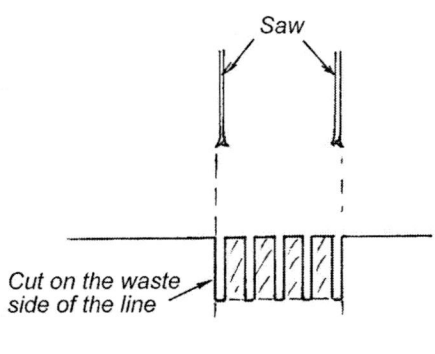

Saw

Cut on the waste side of the line

Fig 24.

E. Using the widest chisels possible start from one side of the joint with the chisel 1/8" (3mm) from the top and with the chisel angled slightly upwards as shown. Carefully chisel towards the centre of the piece of wood. Come down the side until you are within 1/8" (3mm) of the bottom. Then do the same from the other side, always working towards the centre of the wood (Figure 25). This will leave you with a small hill in the centre of the wood and you can now clear this out by chiselling horizontally from the top finally going right the way down to the bottom. You will almost certainly find it easier to chisel the wood from one side, rather than from the other because of the grain of the wood and therefore you should always do most of your chiselling from the easier side.

F. The second piece of wood is marked out in much the same way as the first piece. For

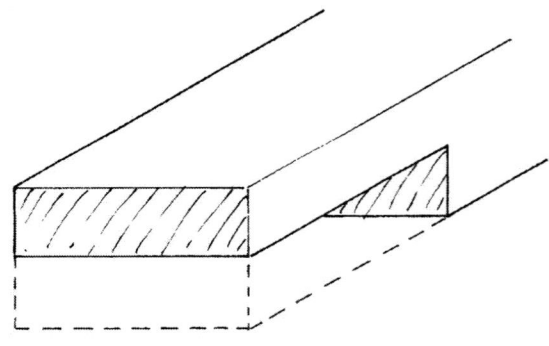

Fig 26.

G. If your joint does not fit together then use the saw and chisel to carefully pare waste material until it fits snugly.

The inside of the joint should always be left rough giving a good mechanical bond with the glue that is used, so do not clean it up with sandpaper and files. If you can do a simple Tee Halving joint then you can do any

28

of the other joints. However, you will find that the halving joint will cover most of the joints that you will need to do. For instance, the wood filleting (cleats) attached to a plywood bulkhead/frame and the inside of the hull (Figure 27).

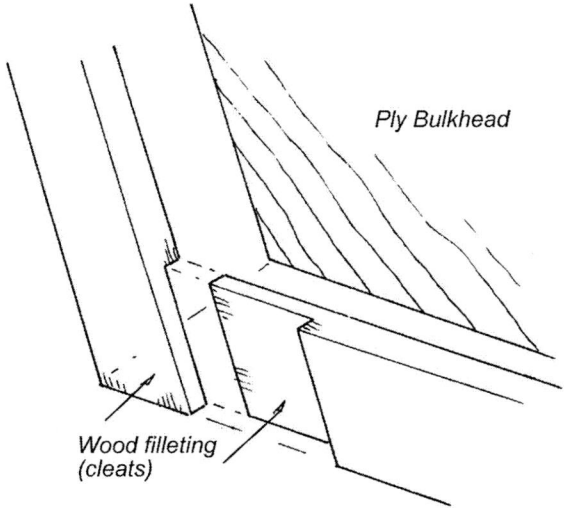

Ply Bulkhead

Wood filleting (cleats)

Fig 27.

You will find some of the other joints useful too, for instance the dovetail halving joint is ideal when you have a piece of timber which is subjected to a force along it's length trying to pull it away from the piece of timber to which it is being joined. If you look at this joint you will see that if you try and pull the joint to the right then you will be pulling against the shape of the dovetail itself which resists the joint coming apart (Figure 28).

The bridle joint is good for making up frame work or doors and also for letting fillets into corner posts etc. The finger (or comb joint) is a simplified form of the traditional dovetail joint but because all the fingers are square it is actually very simple to do and yet, very strong. If you are unfamiliar with the use of joinery tools etc then it is always a good idea to make a practice joint on pieces of scrap wood before you actually attack your boat.

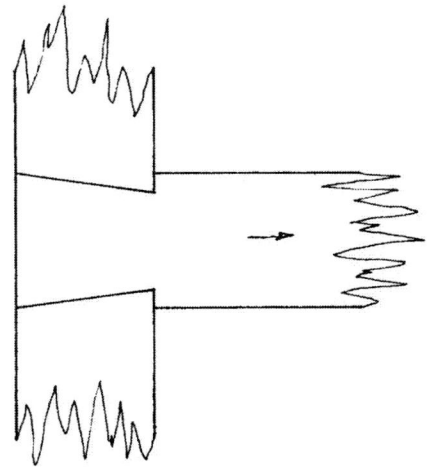

Fig 28.

The one thing to remember with joints is that the joints should be positioned and designed to give the maximum possible gluing area as well as the maximum possible mechanical bond between the two components. Sometimes you will not be able to use some of the joints, perhaps because it is too awkward. For instance deck beams are often let into the inwale and deck carlin by using a variant on the tee halving joint which I tend to call angle halving (Figure 29).

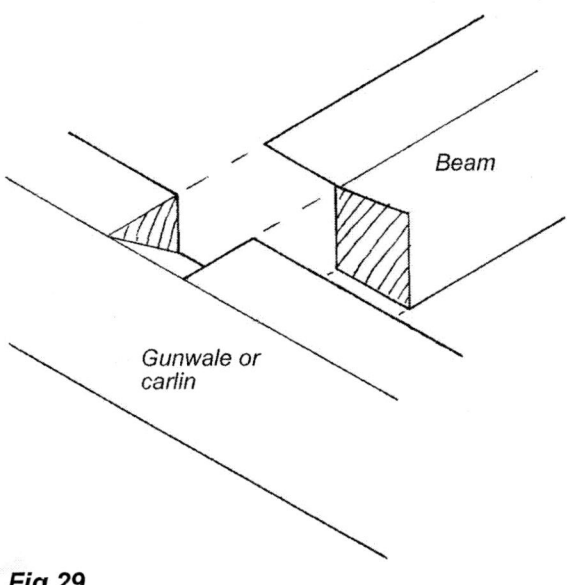

Beam

Gunwale or carlin

Fig 29.

You will notice that I have not mentioned mortice and tenon joints or grooved haunch joints etc. These are all excellent joints to use but there is never any need to go quite that far unless you delight in the construction of that sort of joint. Should you require any further information on the construction of simple joints there are many DIY publications on the market which go through most joints in a step by step sequence.

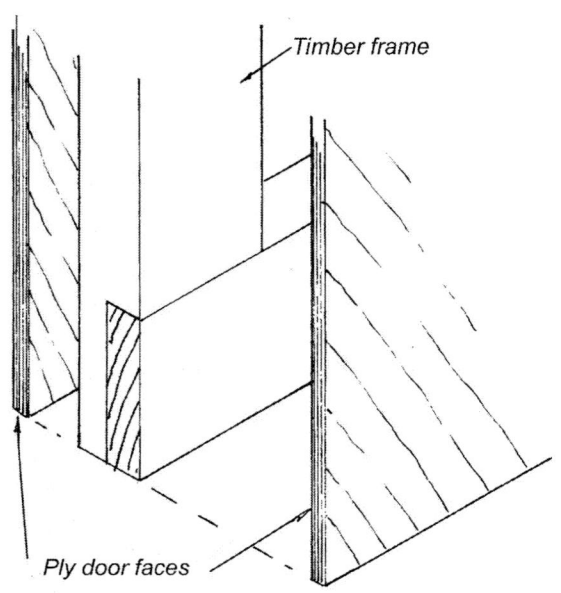

Fig 30. **Corner halving joint used instead of the more traditional mortice and tenon for door frames.**

3.1.2 The Scarf Join

The scarf is a useful joint for joining pieces of timber together to make up longer lengths and for joining plywood sheets to make up the plank length. It is a strong join with plenty of faying (gluing) surface. It's length is usually between 6 to 8 times the thickness of the timber being joined. Figure 31 shows the simple (plain) scarf used for joining lengths of plank—the other two examples, lipped and hooked scarfs are sometimes used for joining specific components (ie., keels, deck covering boards etc).

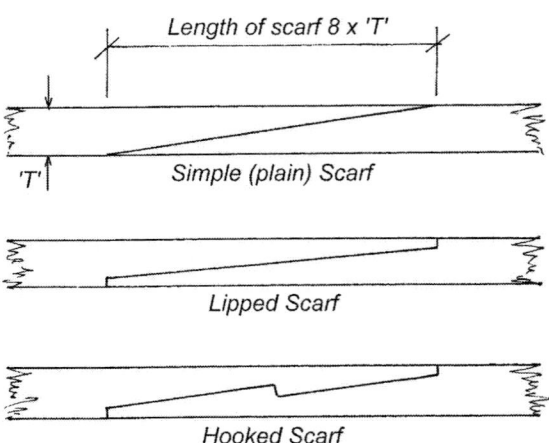

Fig 31. **Scarf Joints.**

If you have a lot of scarfs to do because you cannot get timber suitable for stringers etc in one length then a scarfing jig is a useful tool to have. There all sorts of sophisticated scarf cutting jigs you can buy, but this one, in Figure 32 is a cheap alternative and very effective – it is much like a mitre box.

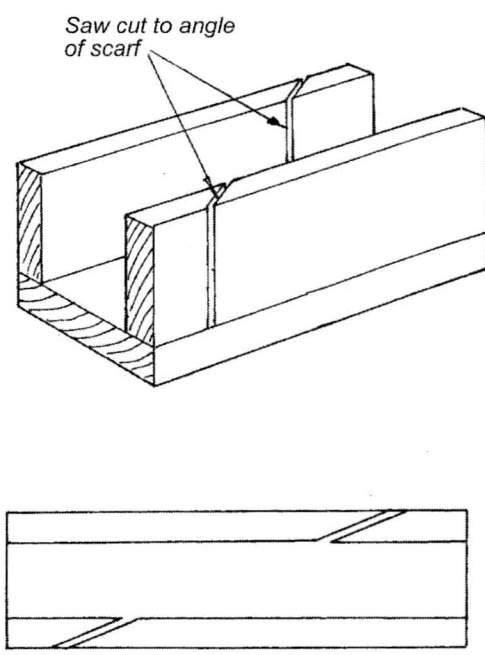

Fig 32. **Scarfing Box.**

Alternatively, you can set up a bench saw with the correct scarfing angle set up on the table guide.

3.1.3 Solid Wood Joints for Chines

The advantage of solid wood chines (chine stringers), is that they give you something to screw the ply skin too and greatly add to the hull's longitudinal strength, perhaps more so than with a simple epoxy join.

Generally speaking, solid wood chines are used in boats where the plywood hull skin is applied over-size to the framework and trimmed – ie., the ply hull skin is not pre-shaped. However, solid wood chines can be used in the construction of boats with pre-shaped (computer generated) hull skin planking too – the 'V' gap which forms between the edges of the ply hull skin over the chines is often simply filled with solid wood or thickened epoxy.

There are several points to consider when fitting chine stringers. The first is, that on larger boats, trying to fit them in one piece is a struggle and therefore I prefer to fit them in several pieces by laminating them in situ (Figure 33).

If you have tried to fit a chine stringer (or, for that matter, an inwale (gunwale) stringer) in one piece and it proves too difficult to bend into shape, especially at the bow, simply run it though with a long saw cut, in the difficult area, so that you can then bend it round in 2 or more pieces (Figure 34).

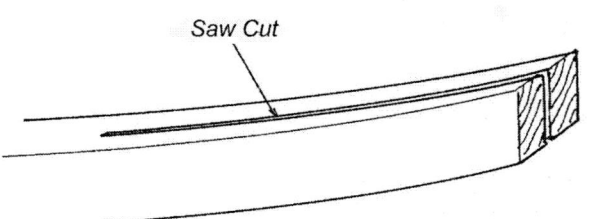

Saw Cut

Fig 34. Saw cut stringer making it easier to bend into shape.

A second point to consider is how you are going to attach the stringers to the ends of the boat. The stringer has to lie flush with the rest of the framework in order to allow the planking to fit properly and so, at the stem it either has to be let in flush with the stem by sinking it into a slot or, it has to butt against the aft side of the inner stem post using some kind of bracket or block to attach it to the post (Figure 35).

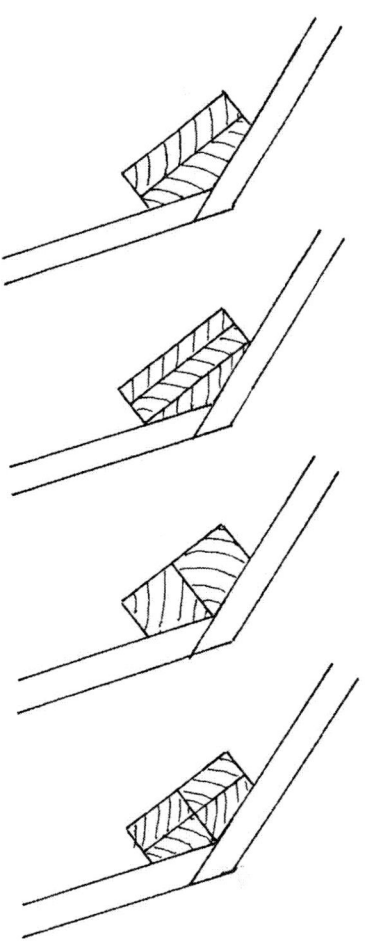

Fig 33. Laminated Chine Stringers.

just butt against the stem post or, if there is a ply fore and aft girder, they are chamfered to fit against it (Figure 36).

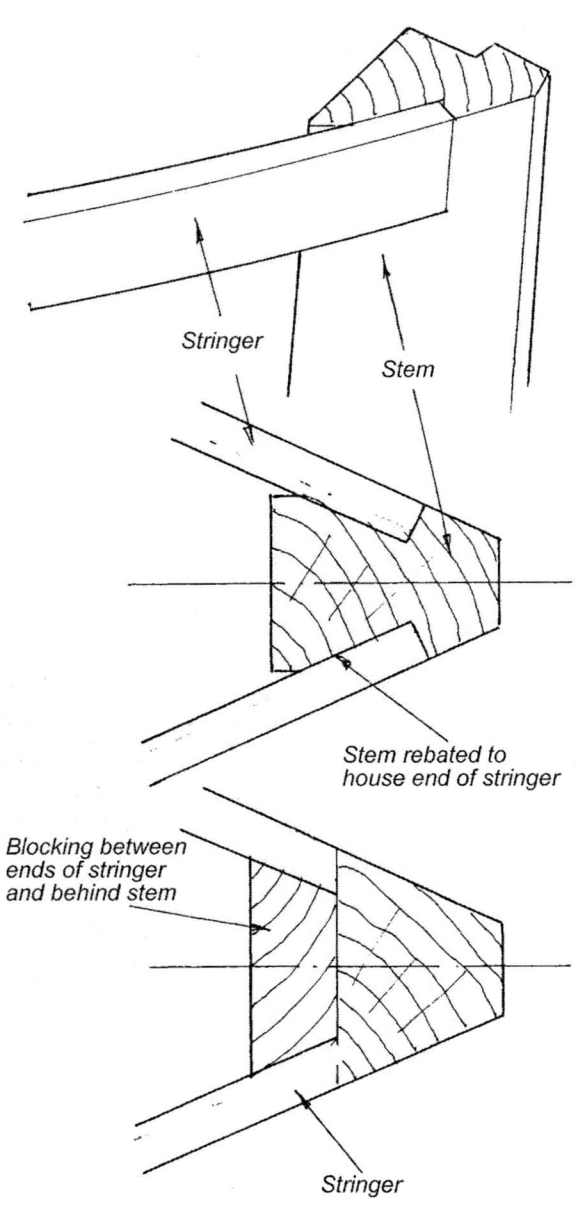

Stringer

Stem

Stem rebated to house end of stringer

Blocking between ends of stringer and behind stem

Stringer

Fig 35. Two ways of attaching stringers to the inner stem.

I prefer to cut it into a slot, although sometimes, down at the foot of the stem (the forefoot), there is not enough width in the inner stem to take a pair of slots for the port and starboard stringers and a compromise needs to be made – very often the stringers

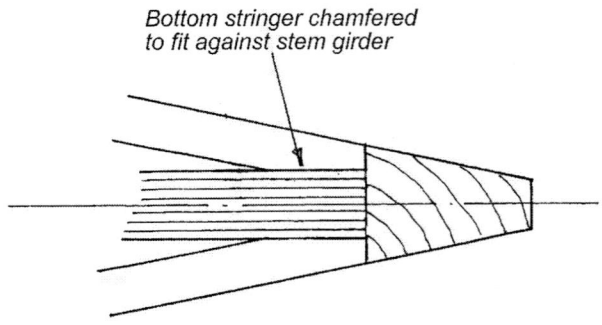

Bottom stringer chamfered to fit against stem girder

Fig 36. Lowest stringer fitted into girder.

Assuming the transom has a frame around it's forward face, the stringers need to be fitted into slots cut into the frame but not into the transom itself – the transom covers the ends of the chine stringer (Figure 37).

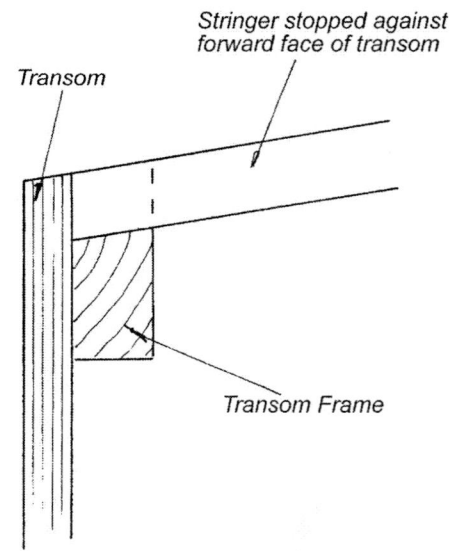

Stringer stopped against forward face of transom

Transom

Transom Frame

Fig 37. 'Normal' stringer connection to the transom with the transom covering the ends of the stringers.

This can be an awkward slot to make because the transom is in the way of being able to use a saw to cut through the frame and therefore what some builders do, is to cut the slot right through the transom and to cover the ends of the stringers with a thin layer of ply (an outer transom) which is fitted before planking starts.

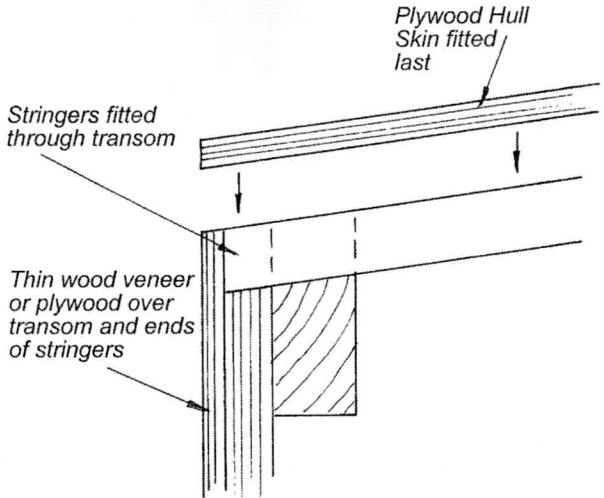

Fig 38. The transom cut through by the stringers for an easier formed join and a thin veneer/ply added to cover the ends of the stringers.

3.2 Epoxy Joints for Frame Construction

We will look at epoxy joints for the general framework first and then move onto epoxy joints for the chine seams.

3.2.1 Replacing Wood Fillets with Epoxy

Wood fillets between ply girders and bulkheads can often be replaced with epoxy fillets (Figure 39). This usually makes construction quicker and easier.

The design should specify the size and type (low-high density) of epoxy fillet to be used, but as a general guide for bonding plywood

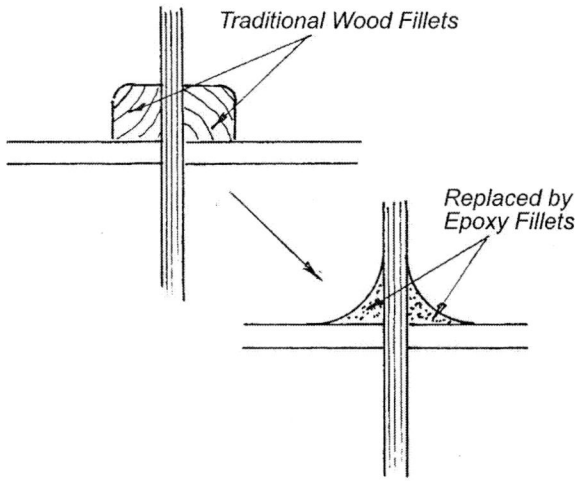

Fig 39. Simple epoxy fillets replacing solid wood fillets.

components other than those around highly stressed areas (centreboard cases etc), the general rule is that the radius of the fillet is 3 times the maximum thickness of plywood being joined. So if you are bonding 3/8" (9mm) thick plywood then the radius of the fillet would be just over 1" (27mm) – see Figure 8.

For more highly stressed areas, the fillet would be used in combination with glass re-inforcing tape (Figure 40).

I find that if you let the thickened epoxy fillet go off before applying the glass re-inforcing, you get air strapped underneath. The best way, I find, and the way that gives the best chemical bond within the join, is to apply the thickened fillet as cleanly as possible, remove any excess epoxy and then apply the tape straight away. This means that the epoxy fillet under the glass re-inforcing has not set solid to leave dips and gulleys that trap air. If you get it right, the epoxy fillet is starting to harden and therefore will not flatten out when applying the tape but is pliable enough to be 'mouldable' in getting rid of dips that can trap air.

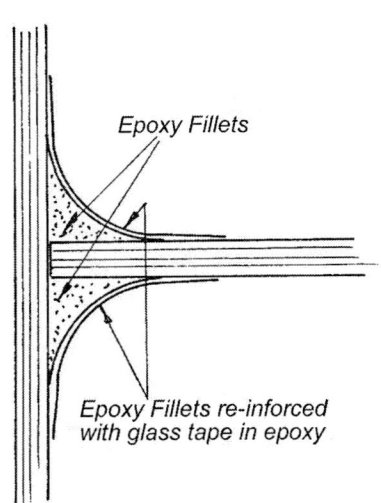

Fig 40. Epoxy fillets re-inforced with glass tape.

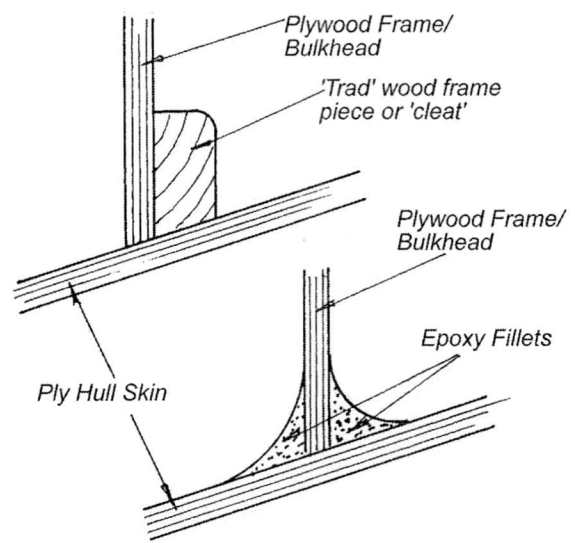

Fig 41. Epoxy fillets replacing wood fillets (cleats) at the hull/frame join.

3.2.2 Replacing Wood With Epoxy Joints Between the Plywood Frames/Bulkheads and Hull Skin

Instead of having a solid wood fillet or 'cleat' around the edge of the ply frame/bulkhead to which the planking is attached, you can simply have epoxy fillets which are quick and easy to apply (Figure 41).

The disadvantage of epoxy fillets in this area is that, using large quantities of epoxy is expensive and also, if the fillets are applied too small, you can end up with a 'crease' running down the plywood planking on the outside of the hull because there is not enough bearing surface between a main structural frame/bulkhead and the hull. This usually only happens where a thin ply skin is used but once this 'hard spot' occurs, there is not much you can do about it (Figure 42).

Having a wood fillet/cleat or frame around the edge of the plywood frame may in some cases spread any load transmitted to the hull skin from the frame, better. Note—do check

with the designer first, if you are replacing wood fillets with epoxy—or the other way around and replacing epoxy with wood fillets.

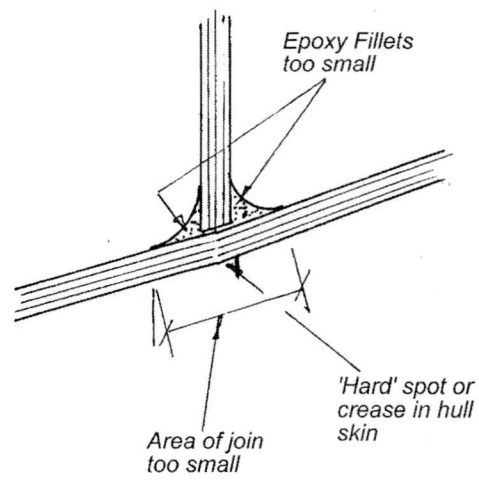

Fig 42. Hard spots and creases caused by epoxy filleted joins which are too small.

3.2.3 Epoxy Joints for Chine Seams

If you use epoxy chine joins we assume that the plywood hull panels are pre-shaped (the shapes are given on the plans). There are 2 or 3 ways of making up an epoxy chine joint, each with it's advantages and disadvantages.

3.2.3.1 The Simple Epoxy/Glass Chine Join

The straight epoxy/glass join is the simplest and quickest type of epoxy chine but also uses the most epoxy. The design specification will tell you how big the join should be and how many layers of glass re-inforcing to use. Figure 43 shows a typical chine join for a boat of around 24' (7.3m).

The way I tackle this type and size of join is to do as much preparation as possible before mixing any epoxy. First, clean the join making sure that the surfaces are clean and clear of any dirt, dust and loose wood fibres etc. second, tape up any gaps on the outside so that epoxy does not drop right through and onto the floor!

The third job is to prepare the glass re-inforcing. This may simply be a standard width of woven glass tape on a roll. I lay it

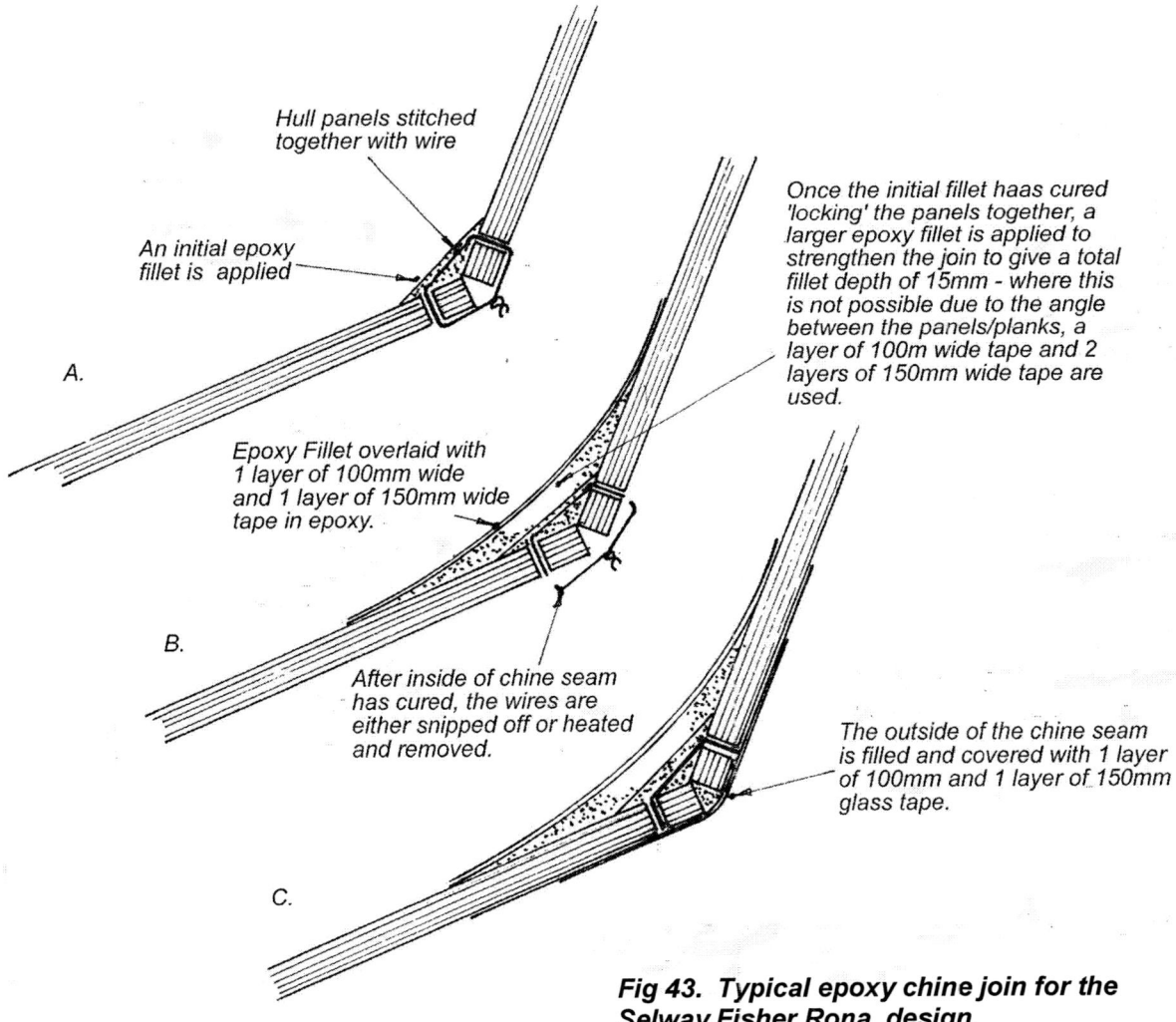

Hull panels stitched together with wire

An initial epoxy fillet is applied

A.

Once the initial fillet haas cured 'locking' the panels together, a larger epoxy fillet is applied to strengthen the join to give a total fillet depth of 15mm - where this is not possible due to the angle between the panels/planks, a layer of 100m wide tape and 2 layers of 150mm wide tape are used.

Epoxy Fillet overlaid with 1 layer of 100mm wide and 1 layer of 150mm wide tape in epoxy.

B.

After inside of chine seam has cured, the wires are either snipped off or heated and removed.

The outside of the chine seam is filled and covered with 1 layer of 100mm and 1 layer of 150mm glass tape.

C.

Fig 43. Typical epoxy chine join for the Selway Fisher Rona design.

out over the join and cut to length before folding it carefully and draping it over the gunwale close to where I am going to start laying it down. If there is more than one layer of re-inforcing and especially if the layers have different widths and are to go on, in a certain sequence, make sure that you can clearly identify them by attaching a piece of masking tape and marking them.

Now some unthickened epoxy can be mixed and applied as a primer coat to the chine surfaces that will take the join material. I allow this to cure, but not for too long before I apply the epoxy fillet – this is made up from thickened epoxy using the resin/hardners plus microfibres, microballoons and colloidal silica (the design or epoxy manufacturer's manual should give an indication of the correct mix). The size and/or depth of the fillet will be specified. Apply the fillet as

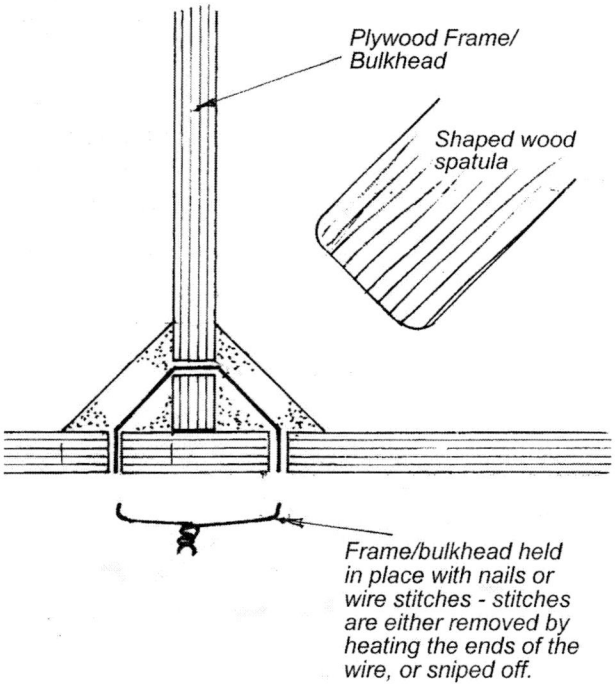

Plywood Frame/ Bulkhead

Shaped wood spatula

Frame/bulkhead held in place with nails or wire stitches - stitches are either removed by heating the ends of the wire, or sniped off.

Fig 44. Make up spatula to suit the size and shape of epoxy fillet being applied—this example is from the Selway Fisher Lynx 14 design and is square ended rather than the more usual semi-circle shape.

cleanly as possible using a spatula of the correct size and shape to give the size of fillet you want (Figure 44).

I then apply the glass re-inforcing before the epoxy fillet is fully cured – lay the re-inforcing onto the fillet using a small split washer roller to smooth it gently down onto the filler and to push air from under the re-inforcing. Once the tape is in place, brush unthickened epoxy resin onto the tape to "wet" it out – you will see the 'wetting' process as the tape changes in colour from a silvery/white to translucent.

Keep a sharp eye out for any trapped bubbles and use the roller to get rid of them. Whilst the first re-inforcing layer of glass is curing, apply the next layer, repeating the process. Don't over use the resin or you will end up with epoxy runs everywhere – you should find that there is sufficient resin between the layers to wet out the final layer without too much additional resin being applied.

No matter which method is used for the epoxy chine seams, make sure that you work symmetrically (both sides at the same time) and check regularly to make sure that there are no twists in the framework – once the chines cure, there is no way to remove any twist. If the centreline seam is epoxied, do this first followed by the next chine seams up – work on each pair of chine seams together.

Getting a smooth finish on an epoxy chine join can be messy and arduous with much grinding and sanding needed. To cut this down, use peel ply – this is a polyester cloth which is pressed into the final epoxy coat over the join. The peel ply evens out bumps etc. Once the join has cured, the peel ply is removed leaving a surface that usually needs little sanding and grinding to get a good finish.

3.2.3.2 The Combi Epoxy/Wood Chine Join

I have used this join successfully on a number of boats up to 25' (7.3m) in length but there is no reason why this method cannot be used on larger craft. With this join, a rectangular, or more often a square wood stringer is fitted so that one of it's surfaces bears against one of the ply hull skins being joined at the chine.

One of the ply hull panels is glued and fastened to the stringer and the adjacent hull panel is temporarily fastened in place either

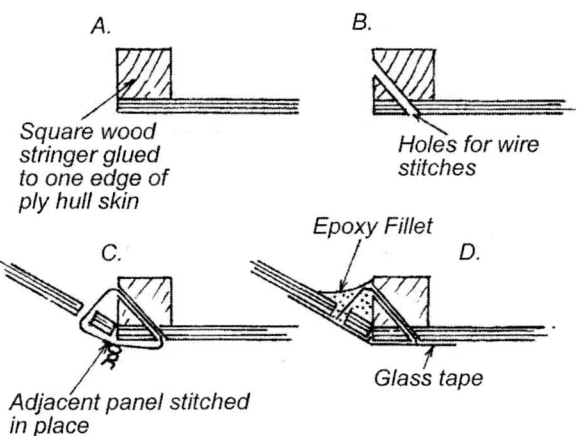

Fig 45. A simple combi epoxy/wood stringer.

using stitches as shown in Figure 45, or temporary nails. The seam is then primed with unthickened epoxy and then filled with thickened epoxy.

This method uses less epoxy and adds stiffness to the structure before the chine seam is made which can be an advantage.

3.2.3.3 The Edge Girder Chine Method

I have seen this used on quite large craft over 35' (10.7m) although it can be used on smaller boats. A slot is cut into the frames to accommodate a wood stringer on edge. This method is best suited to long thin hulls where the curve subjected to the stringers is fairly gentle. If the stringer will not take up the curve in one piece, it will need to be laminated in place.

The edge of the stringer adjacent to the hull panels is chamfered to suit the angles of the framework and the planking is then fitted and epoxy fillets applied either side of the stringer similar to the fillet for the Combi Epoxy/Wood Join.

This is a very stiff form of chine stringer which does not use too much epoxy and which adds considerably to the longitudinal strength of the hull. It is not the easiest form of stringer though and does tend to trap more bilge water etc.

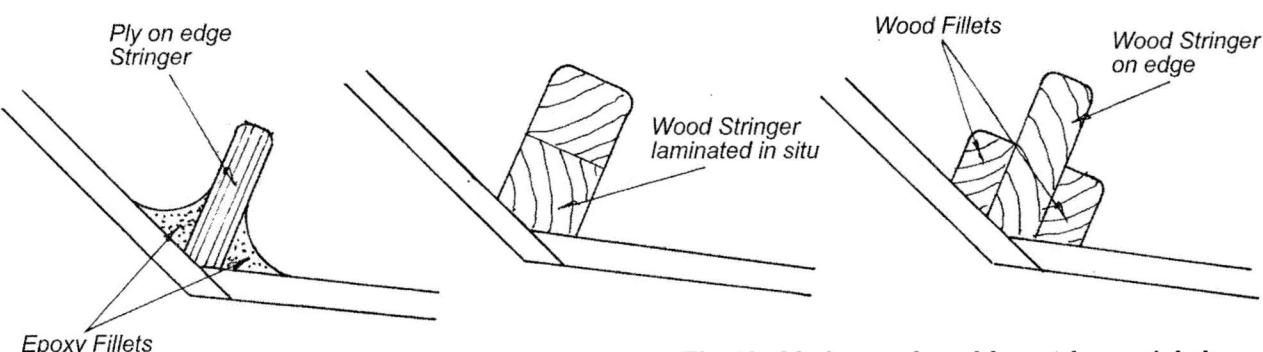

Fig 46. Various edge chine stringers/girders.

Above—the early stages of Graham Young's Selway Fisher Tideway 14 showing the use of halving joins between framing fillets in the cockpit area.

Right—a view of Graham Young's Tideway 14 at a much later stage showing the use of cross halving joins in the wood framing cleats around the companion entrance and the slots taken out of the coachhouse top beams ready for the stringers to be fitted.

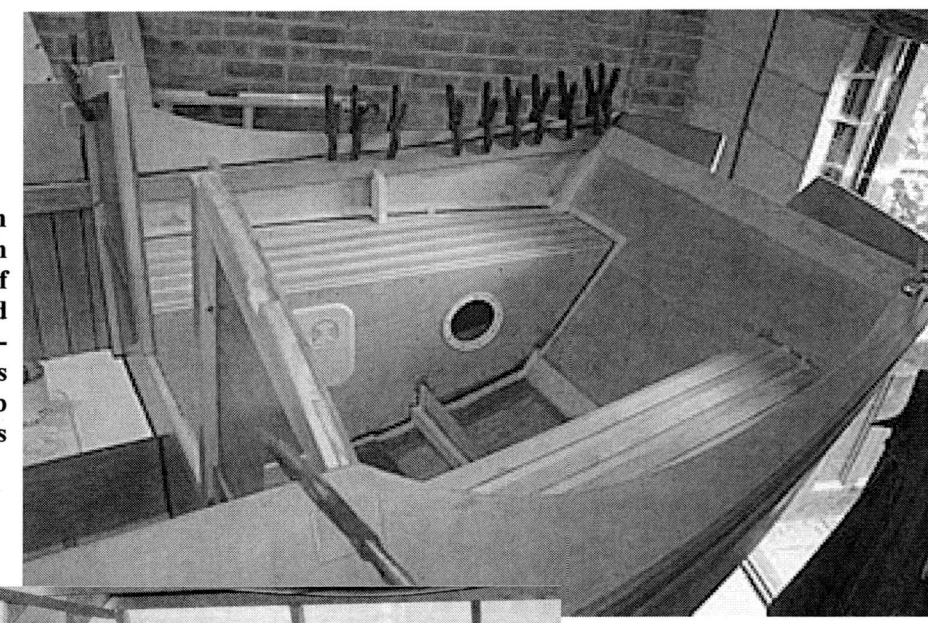

Left—a Selway Fisher Highlander 18 with stitch and tape chine seams—the outside veneer of the plywood planking in-way of the chine seams has been routed away leaving an area in which the outside glass tape will sit and be flush with the plywood plank surface.

Chapter 4

MATERIALS
COMMONLY USED FOR LARGER
PLYWOOD BOATS

The following is limited to a brief discussion of the materials normally used rather than a comparison of all available woods. Some builders will have successfully used other species so use the lists as an initial guide.

4.1 Solid Wood for Frameworks

Timber	Weight Lbs/cu.ft	Weight Kgs/cu.m	Comments
Afrormosia	43	690	Good durable timber, easily worked
Cedar (Western Red)	24	385	Good durable timber, easily worked
Douglas Fir	33	530	Reasonably good but expensive
Iroko (African Teak)	40	640	Very good but heavy and not easy to work – tends to warp in thin laminates – can need special treatment when gluing.
Larch	35	560	Good durable timber
Mahogany (Brazilian)	32	515	Good durable timber
Oak (English)	45	720	Very good but heavy
Oak (American)	48	770	Very good but heavy
Pitch Pine	44	705	Very good but heavy
Pine (British Columbian)	35	560	Reasonably good
Redwood (European)	32	515	Cheap – ok for low cost boats but not very durable unless well sealed
Sitka Spruce	28	450	Varies in density and quality
Teak	41	655	Expensive and not easily worked – needs special treatment when gluing.
Utile	41	655	Very good but heavy

We also have to bring sustainability into the choice of timber we use for frameworks. Looking at the above list I would use Redwood for the timber in framework if the boat being built is to have a minimum cost and for which I was not worried about the resale value. However I would use Cedar,

Douglas Fir or English Oak (of which, at the time of writing, there is plenty) for a higher quality/higher value boat.

4.2 Plywood for Frameworks

When looking at the quality of plywood for frameworks we come up against two often asked questions :-

4.2.1 Can I Use Cheaper Exterior Plywood for the Frames and Bulkheads?

The answer is often yes but with the following caveats. I would always use a good Marine quality plywood for main structural items – centreboard cases, mast support bulkheads and the main companion way bulkhead (which is exposed to the weather on one side anyway).

Exterior WBP (Water and boil proof) plywood is inferior to true good quality Marine plywood in four main ways – first, the quality of wood used for the veneers is often lower than that used for Marine plywood (less durable and less strong). Second, the veneers are not of equal thickness – you will often find that an Exterior grade plywood has paper thin external veneers and thick bulk core veneers, which makes it less strong and less durable. Third you will find that the glues and bonding between the veneers is of a lower quality and therefore Exterior plywood is more likely to delaminate under compression and if water enter the plywood. Finally, there are often voids between the veneers – or even areas where a particular veneer overlaps where it stops and starts, leading to a bump right across the plywood.

So, be cautious where you use Exterior plywood – using it for bunk fronts, interior

joinery, lesser structural bulkheads etc is fine, unless you are trying to keep the cost right down and use it for everything. From a resale point of view, it will be easier to be able to say that the whole boat is built of Marine grade plywood, especially if you have a sample of the plywood with the BS1088 stamp and Kite Mark on it.

4.2.2 If I Sheath the Boat Can I Use Exterior Plywood for the Hull Planks/Panels?

Again, yes but keep in mind the comments in 4.2.1 above. I use glass sheathing (epoxy and woven glass cloth) to help protect the hull, especially from scratches and marine borers. I do not use it to make up for the use of poorer quality plywood. The glass will back up a low quality outside veneer and add a small amount to the overall strength and stiffness of the hull (unless hybrid cloths are used which would considerably add to the strength but be very expensive) but you are probably better off overall, using a better quality plywood in the first place.

4.3 Glues and Adhesives

There are several glues and adhesives that I have used for framework construction. This is not a definitive list and trade names will vary around the world.

Do not be tempted to use the PVA glues which say they are for exterior use – they are no good for marine use. If you have doubts over a particular glue on the market, contact the manufacturers/suppliers for their recommendations rather than risk using them.

GLUE/ADHESIVE	COMES AS	COMMENTS
Cascamite (Extramite)	White powder to be mixed with water	Can be brittle and does not like total immersion in water – use for interior joinery only
Aerolite 306	2 part – a white powder to be mixed with water and a formic/ascetic acid	Very durable and can be used for gap filling – excellent for frameworks
Cascophen Resorcinal	2 part – often a brown and powder hardener	Very durable and excellent for frameworks
Balcotan (Polyurethane)	Single shot – straight out of the tube – no mixing	Cures on contact with the moisture in the wood – very durable and easy to clean up and use – components being glued must be clamped as it foams – excellent for frameworks but has a very definite shelf life once a tube is opened.
Marine epoxy resins (WEST, SP etc)	Resin and hardener often in a 5:1 mix	Very strong when thickened as a glue – difficult to clean up when hardened and expensive.

4.4 Fastenings

4.4.1 Screws

4.4.1.1 Steel

Steel screws will rust and should therefore not be used – even if they are totally buried and covered – the moisture in the wood can make them corrode. I do however, use them for initial fastening if I am using brass screws in the final construction. Brass screws are not particularly strong and have a tendency to sheer which can be very frustrating so, I initially use steel screws to fasten the wood components together whilst the glue cures. I then remove the steel screws and replace them with the brass screws.

4.4.1.2 Brass

Brass screws are the most commonly available for marine use. But I only use brass for general interior joinery and for use under water only if the hull is sheathed. The zinc in the brass can leach out leaving the screw very weak.

4.4.1.3 Stainless Steel

Available in two grades – A2 for above the water and A4 for use under water. There are arguments about their use in a marine environment as stainless steel can degrade badly but if they are covered and sheathed over, I have never had a problem.

4.4.1.4 Silicon Bronze

Excellent but expensive so I use only in the most exposed and stressed areas of the hull.

4.4.2 Gripfast Nails

These are barbed ring nails with excellent holding power - the type used in the marine industry are bronze and they come in sizes from 5/8" (15mm) to around 3" (75mm) long and in various different gauges. All but the smallest require a pilot hole but they are quick and simple to use when fastening plywood to solid timber framing.

4.4.3 Other Fastenings

4.4.3.1 Carriage Bolts

These come in a variety of materials (although usually mild steel) and sizes – they have a domed head with a small length of square shank just below the head which prevents them from turning when tightening them up. I usually drill a slightly undersized hole when fitting them and hammer them through. They are excellent for major construction joints – ie., engine beds, anything that is through bolted etc.

4.4.3.2 Coach Screws

Rather like a large screw and for use on large structural items where a through bolt fitting is impractical – ie., some floor fastenings, knees etc. They are usually mild steel and sometimes galvanised and have a square or hexagonal head and come with a very course thread with great gripping power.

4.4.3.3 Machine Screws

Often stainless steel but also bronze and brass – they have a variety of different heads but are often raised or domed countersunk. They are threaded for the entire length of the shank which is not tapered so that they are rather like bolts with continuous threads. They are often used for deck fittings etc but not for items under stress such as keel bolts where the continuous thread weakens the bolt/screw.

4.4.3.4 Threaded Rod

Continuously threaded rod – usually stainless steel with no head. This can be very useful for long fastenings and is fine to use in areas where there is not a lot of stress.

4.4.3.5 Dumps and Drift Bolts

These are 'blind' fastenings (not through fastenings) like large nails – they are usually mild steel and slightly tapered with a domed head and fitted in a slightly under size hole. They are very rarely used now but were often incorporated around the deadwood/skeg where through bolts were awkward, especially when there was a stern tube in the way.

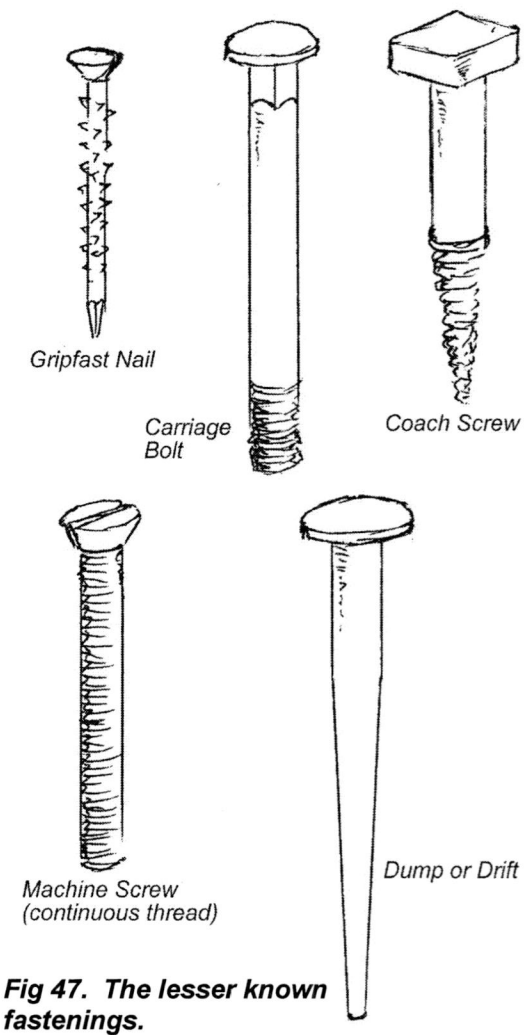

Gripfast Nail

Carriage Bolt

Coach Screw

Machine Screw (continuous thread)

Dump or Drift

Fig 47. The lesser known fastenings.

Finally, when considering the correct material to use for fastenings, electrolytic corrosion must also be taken into account— see our Manual of Boat Fit-Out.

Chapter 5

SETTING UP THE FRAMEWORK

When erecting and setting up your framework, the one word to remember is 'symmetry'. At all times, whilst fitting a component to one side of the framework, fit the matching component to the other side at the same time. So, when fitting the inwale to the port side, fit the inwale to the starboard side at the same time, otherwise it is almost definite, that you will pull the framework out of 'true'.

Check for square-ness and any twist at all times. Once the inwale goes on and chine stringers (if they are fitted), the framework shape is locked and twists will be permanent.

I have worked on boats in such confined spaces that I have had to work on one side and then slide the hull across the shed so that I could work on the other side – but even here, do not be tempted to fit the inwale and all the chine stringers to one side before working on the other side.

For the purposes of setting up we will assume that you are building the hull upside down. As mentioned in Chapter 2, there are 2 reference lines or planes – the Centreline and the Datum Line (see Figure 15) used in setting the framework up and we now need to reproduce these lines in our building space.

First, we will set up the Reference or Datum Line/Plane. This is a horizontal line or plane from which all vertical dimensions are taken. The most convenient Reference/datum Line is the surface of an exactly horizontal and flat building floor. But, not all building surfaces are truly flat or horizontal and we may not have a proper building floor at all but be building on a mud floor! It is possible to build on a mud or non made up surface but I would always try to build a floor, no matter how temporary before I started (see Figure 14).

On the drawings, the Reference/Datum Line may be a Water Line passing through the hull and if this is the case and we have a good flat building floor, we only need to take our vertical measurements from the building floor adding the distance between the Reference/Datum Line and the building floor

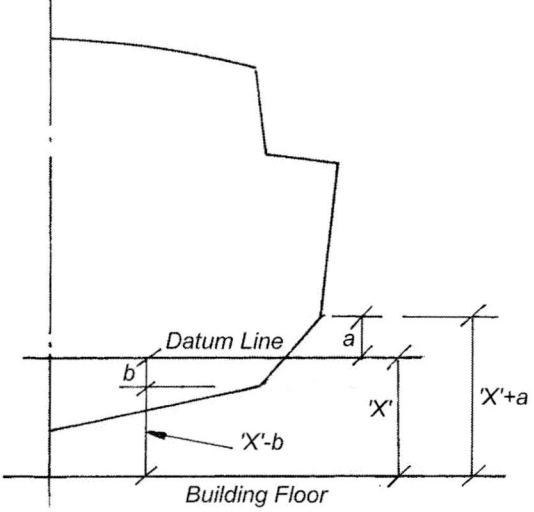

Fig 48. Height measurements taken from a level building floor—shifted from the Datum Line.

for measurements above the Reference/Datum Line or subtracting them if they are below it (Figure 48).

If the floor is not flat or horizontal, you can set up a reference line with a good straight piece of timber and use the edge of this to take measurements from. Modern 'laser' levels make this process much easier – they are not expensive and worth considering. It all depends on how extensive the framework is – a modern plywood 'egg-box' type frame work will have inherent stiffness and, as you slot and assemble the components together and match up the horizontal reference lines you have marked onto the plywood components, the framework is quite easily set up to be level – but even here, make sure that your ply egg-box framework does not sag in the middle by checking the straightness and level of the Reference/Datum Line as it goes through the framework, against a reference edge or surface (Figure 49).

If the framework is more 'traditional', with only transverse frames and laminated hog etc, you will have to check the height of each component against a 'common' reference line or surface.

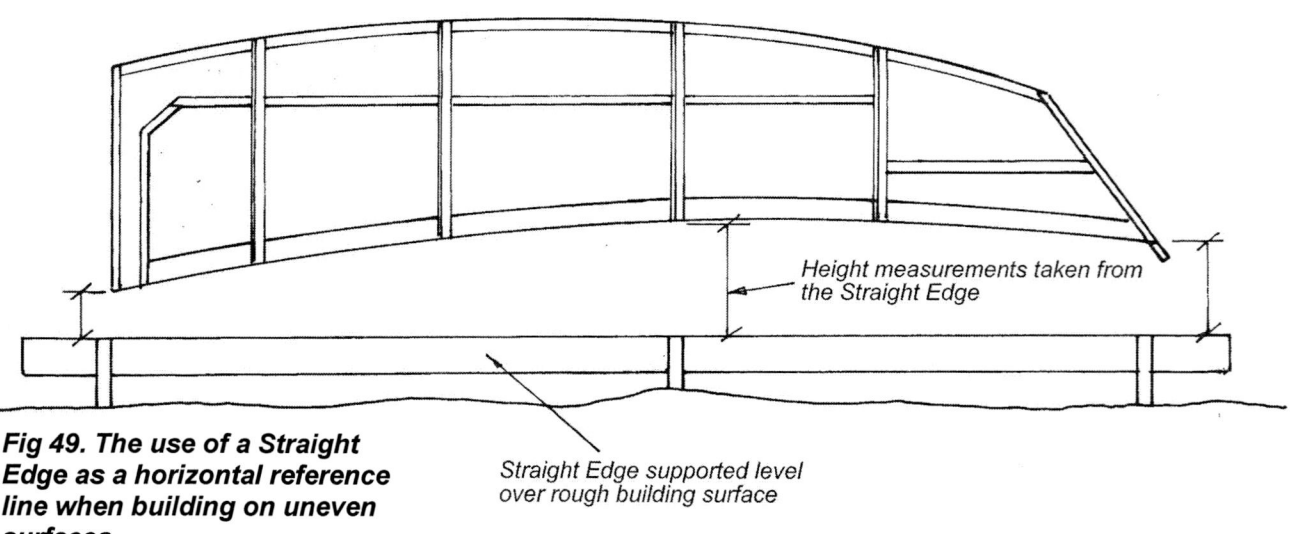

Fig 49. The use of a Straight Edge as a horizontal reference line when building on uneven surfaces.

Height measurements taken from the Straight Edge

Straight Edge supported level over rough building surface

With the modern egg-box framework, make sure that the structure is well supported and check any vertical measurements given on the plan with the building set-up. For instance, the 'peak' of the stem/bow and the bottom of the transom are often given as vertical measurements from the Datum/Reference Line and these should be checked.

The other reference line or plane is of course the centreline of the hull. Here, a modern laser beam level is useful for setting up a straight line from bow to stern on the building floor. Plumb Bob's suspended from the top of the bow and the centre of the transom and from the centre line of each frame will check that the hull is untwisted (Figure 50).

Once you are happy that your framework is 'true', you can start to think about fitting any longitudinal components – hog, inwales, chine stringers etc – and although I have said it before, I will repeat it again – *as you fit these items, fit them symmetrically working on both sides of the hull together and constantly check that the framework remains untwisted.*

See Chapter 3 for the various ways of fitting chine stringers to the stem etc.

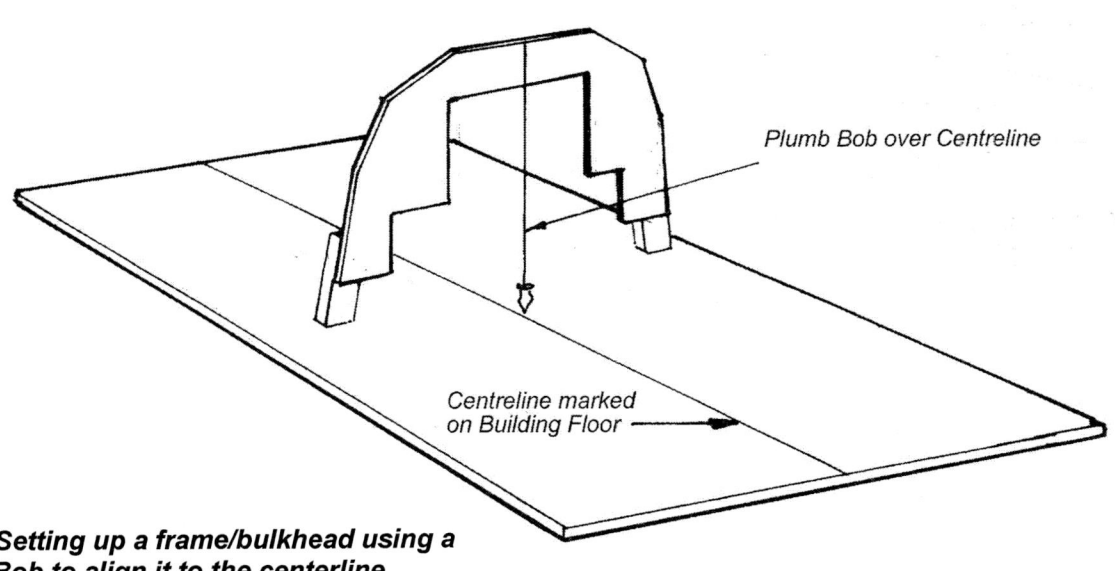

Plumb Bob over Centreline

Centreline marked on Building Floor

Fig 50. Setting up a frame/bulkhead using a Plumb Bob to align it to the centerline.

Above— a Selway Fisher Fanny the Fantail Launch with it's frames set up on a strongback. Note the stem girder. The next items to add are the hog, inwales and chine stringers.
Photo by Peter Chesworth.

Above— a Selway Fisher 17' Evening Swan—the frames and girders have been slotted together to form the basic framework which is supported on a simple strongback. The transom would go on next followed by the gunwale and chine stringers.

Chapter 6

THE PLANKING PROCESS

6.1 Preparing the Framework for planking

Essentially the edges of the framework which 'touch' the inside of the plywood planking need to be correctly shaped to fit against the planking. This is quite a simple planning job but it can take time. We will assume that the framework has chine stringers and that the plywood frames/bulkheads have wood 'cleats' or frames/fillets around their edges. These components all have to be beveled to suit the planking as it lies over the framework.

The chine stringers will need to be beveled in two directions to suit the adjacent pieces of plywood plank that meet over the chine and the centreline structure (hog/inner keel etc) will need to be beveled in much the same way.

The first job is to mark, with a good black line, the 'peak' of the chine stringer or hog where the plywood planks will meet (Figure 51).

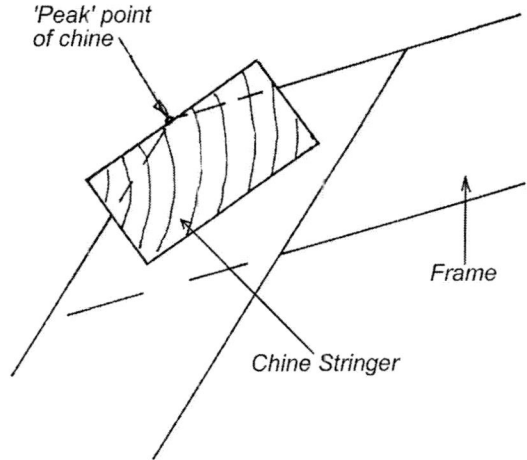

Fig 51. 'Peak' point of chine stringer where the inside surfaces of the ply hull skin meet.

47

To do this we find the 'peak' at each frame/chine crossing by using the frames as a guide to bevel the stringers and make 'valleys' (Figure 52).

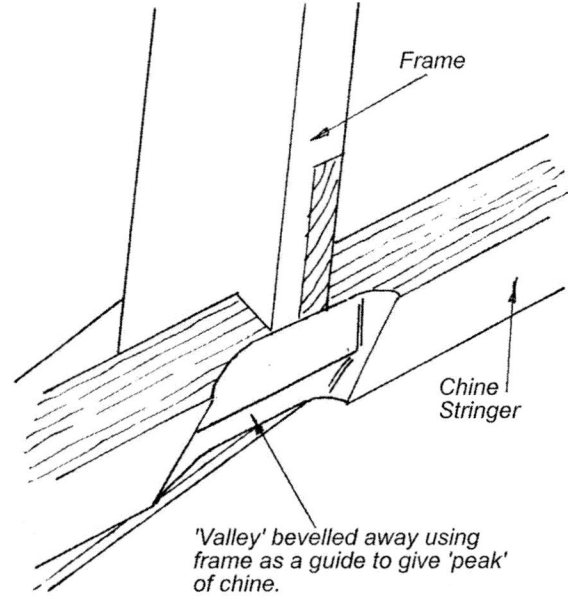

Fig 52. The start of planing up the framework ready to take the planking.

Having cut these valleys, we can carefully plane more valleys on the stringers between the frames using a batten as a guide between adjacent stringers and then plane between them to bevel the entire length of the stringer/hog etc.

The 'cleats' or fillets around the edges of the plywood frames/bulkheads can also be planed to suit the run of the chine stringers, inwale and hog (Figure 53).

If you overdo the planing, epoxy will take up any gaps. The process of planning up the framework, although time consuming, is fairly easy except where your plane hits a fastening – *so when fastening chine stringers etc to the frames/bulkheads, take care to keep screws etc away from the areas that will be planed.*

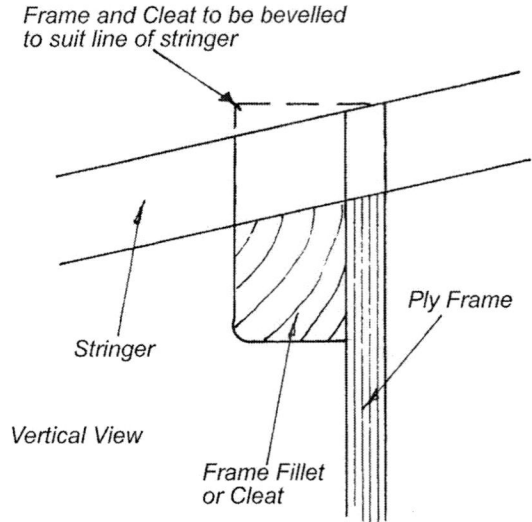

Fig 53. Planing the frames to suit the stringers.

6.2 Planking the Hull (General Notes)

Before we look into the differences between planking Stitch and Tape Hulls and Ply Plank over Frame Hulls there are a couple of important areas to consider. The first is whether the plywood hull planking is put on in just 1 or 2 or more layers.

6.2.1 Multi-layered Plywood Planking

There was a time when a significant factor in the design of a hull for multi-chine plywood construction was whether the surfaces that made up the shape of the hull could be 'conically projected', or not. Theoretically, plywood will bend in one plane at a time – in other words, if you take a sheet of plywood, you can either bend it across it's 4' (1.22m) width *or,* along it's 8' (2.44m) length but *not* both ways at the same time. If you could bend the plywood in both directions at once you would be 'compounding' it and you would end up with the sheet 'dished' (rather like holding up a table cloth horizontally with 4 people trying to stretch it at it's corners – the middle sags or 'dishes' down.

In thin plywood, a certain amount of 'compounding' is possible but it usually has to be forced into the plywood. This can be used on canoes and small dinghies to give what is known as a 'tortured' plywood hull shape. But the amount of 'torturing' you can do and the compound shape you get, is difficult to predict.

So how do you get an attractive curve into the plywood hull shape? – or to tackle the question from the other end – how does the designer check whether the plywood sheets will sit comfortably over the theoretical hull shape? It used to be done by a process called 'conic-projection'.

I am not going to go into 'conic projection' in detail as it is rarely used these days. Basically, although a sheet of plywood can only be bent in one direction at a time, it can, in crude terms, be 'draped' over the surface of a cylindrical cone so that the curve induced in the plywood sheet at one end can change as it goes to the other end and be 'tighter' or more 'relaxed'.

By using 'conic' projection' the designer can dictate where, in mid air, the peak of the cone which relates to the curve of whatever hull panel he/she is checking, is, and work back to make sure that all the points on that hull panel lie on the same cone. The significant area on the surface of the hull is where the shapes of these 'conically projected surfaces 'meet' – that is, at each chine! If the natural chine of one plywood plank surface does not exactly match that of the adjacent plank, you may have problems depending on how big the mis-match is

Having spent many an hour working this out on my drawing board slowly drowning below an ever deepening sea of screwed up paper and card, I often gave up, realizing that a bit

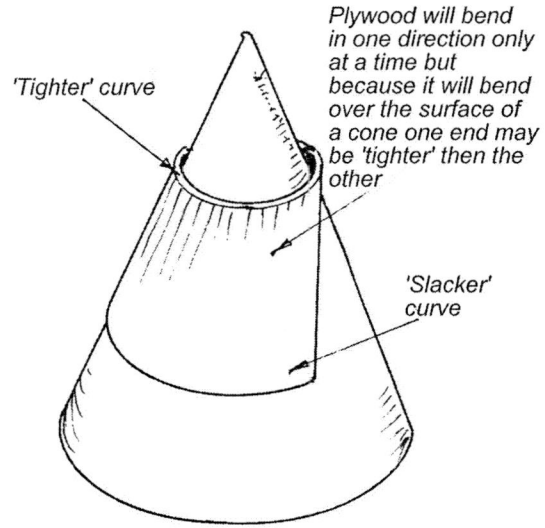

Fig 54. Plywood will only bend in one direction but will lie on the surface of a cone.

of 'forcing' was going to be necessary in order to produce a multi-chine hull which also complied with the 'norms' of good yacht design and efficient hydrodynamics. 'Conic projection' like some basic and cheap yacht CAD programs, limits the curves you can use quite significantly.

Modern yacht CAD programs can go some way to checking that your plywood sheets will lie on the hull surface without significant stress but I often find them unhelpful in this and there are other ways to overcome any difficulties. One way is to use more hull planks/panels (ie. more chines per side) distributing awkward shapes over several narrower planks. The forefoot at the bow is a major problem area as the planking has to bend round towards the bow and twist at the same time from almost horizontal in the centre of the boat to almost vertical at the bow and covering this area with more and narrower planks greatly helps.

The other way is to put each plank on in 2 or more layers of plywood – so a hull skin that has been specified to end up as ½" (12mm) is put on in 2 layers of ¼" (6mm) or 3 layers of 3/16" (4mm) plywood. If you are going to use several layers of plywood the main thing to remember is that you want no voids between the layers so, when you apply the

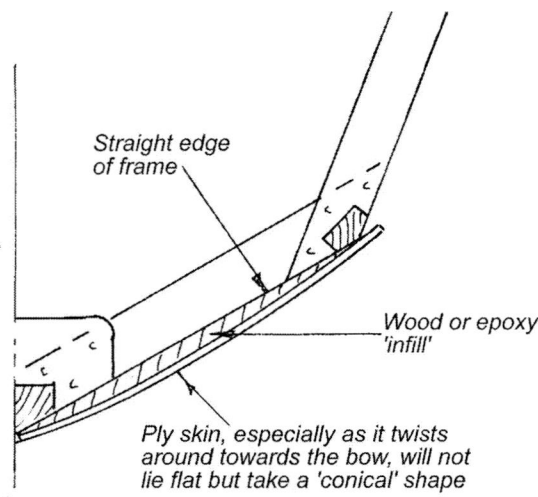

Fig 55. The ply skin will often try to bend away from the framework especially at the forefoot.

second and third layers use plenty of glue (epoxy is best) and use loads of staples to hold the layers in place whilst the glue cures – start stapling from the middle of the panel shape and work out towards the edges chasing any excess glue and air as you go.

You will almost certainly find that as you put the first layer of plywood onto the framework, it will try and 'compound' as it twists round, especially at the forefoot of the bow and it will not lie down nice and flat onto the first frame/bulkhead. Do not worry about this – let it compound but before you finally fix it into place, pack the edge of the frame out to meet it. (Figure 55).

If getting the thinner plywood into place is still difficult, cover the stressed area of plywood with old towels and poor boiling water onto it – this will help make it more supple.

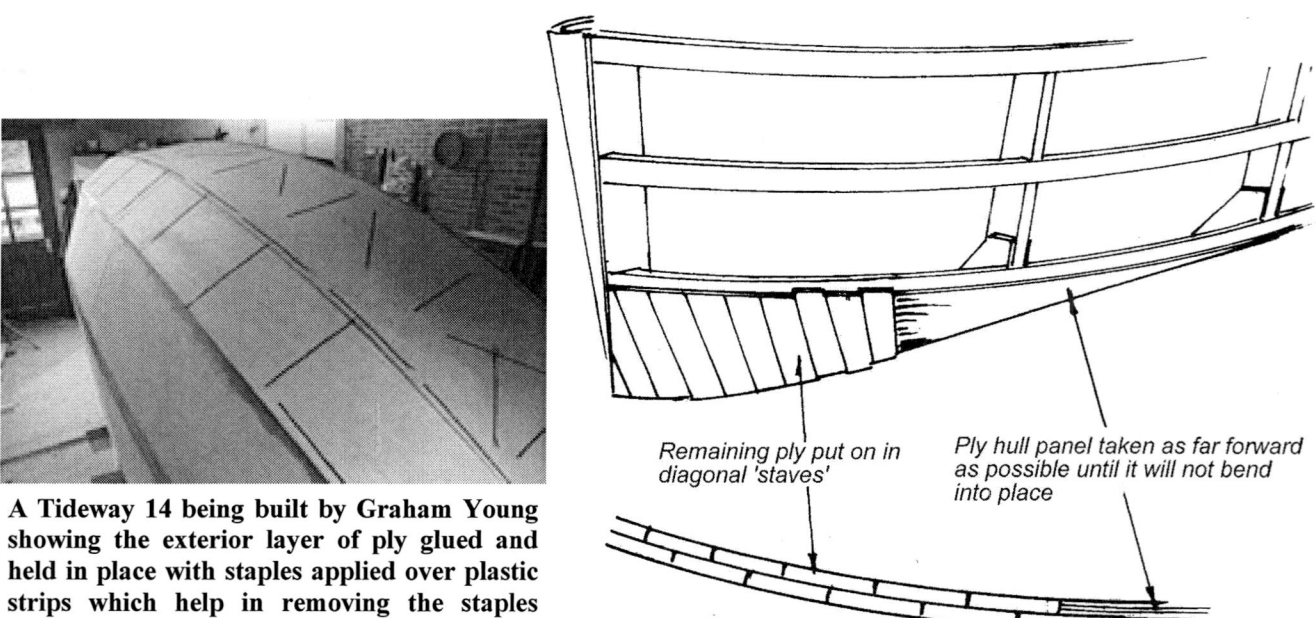

A Tideway 14 being built by Graham Young showing the exterior layer of ply glued and held in place with staples applied over plastic strips which help in removing the staples later.

Fig 56. Fitting part of the hull panel on in diagonal 'staves' where it is too difficult to bend the full panel in place due to the amount of twist in the hull shape.

There have been one or two construction projects that I have been involved in where even putting the plywood panels on in several thin layers was not going to work. In this case I simply stopped the plywood planking as close as I could to the problem area (again, usually the bow forefoot) and put the planking on in the remaining area in 2 or 3 layers of vertical or diagonal strips with plenty of glue (Figure 56).

This is easier to do if you are working to a conventional framework with chine stringers. If you are not and the framework is either non-existent or minimal, you may need to put in some frame work to give yourself something to work too (Figure 57).

Above—the fantail aft end of a Selway Fisher 'Fanny the Fantail' Launch—the inner skin is vertically staved and the outer skin is being applied diagonally.

Below—an illustration taken from the Selway Fisher 23' Ply Canal Cruiser drawings showing the vertically staved bow construction.

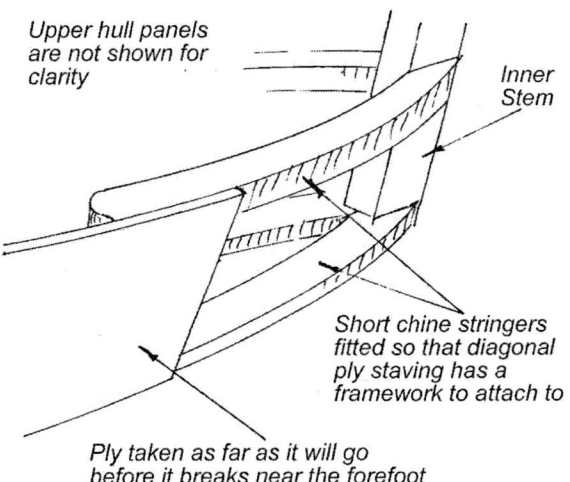

Upper hull panels are not shown for clarity

Inner Stem

Short chine stringers fitted so that diagonal ply staving has a framework to attach to

Ply taken as far as it will go before it breaks near the forefoot

Fig 57. Building in some framework in a stitch and tape hull to take diagonal staving.

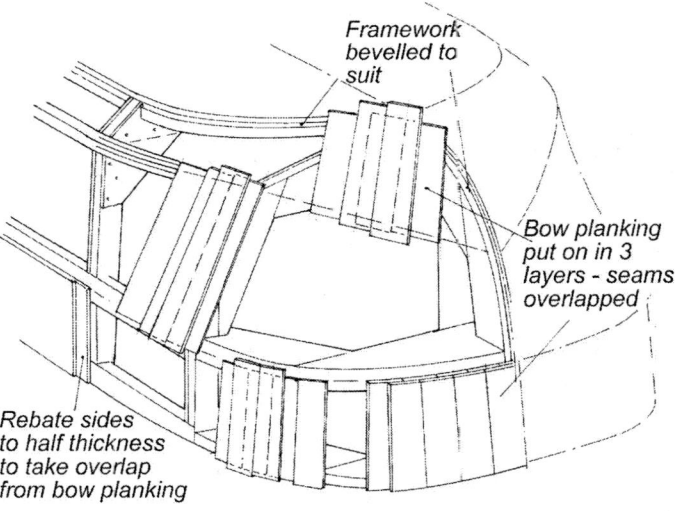

Framework bevelled to suit

Bow planking put on in 3 layers - seams overlapped

Rebate sides to half thickness to take overlap from bow planking

6.2.2 Joining Plywood Plank Lengths

The second important area to consider is how we are going to join the lengths of plywood together to make up the full length of plank. There are several ways to do this but the main methods are either butt straps or scarf joins.

6.2.2.1 Butt Joins

The butt join simply entails 'butting' the edges of the 2 pieces of plywood plank together and backing the join up on the inboard side of the plank with a wood strap. This can be done either 'on' or 'off' the job but is often better done 'off' the job as you have a better chance of getting a join which does not show as a 'kink'. If the butt strap is not wide enough or, if the plank edges are not lying exactly flat against each other, you will end up with 'kink' or hard line (Figure 58).

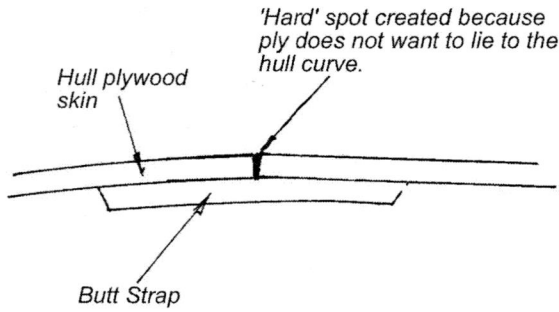

Fig 58. Hard spots created when butt joining planks/panels on the framework.

Making the butt join 'on' the job – ie. making the join with the planks secured to the framework, means that almost certainly the planks are on a curve and not flat and unless you use a substantial butt strap with plenty of fastenings you may not pull the plank edges down enough to avoid a kink. If this is a multi-layered hull with one or more plywood layers going on over the butt, this is not so significant a problem.

If the butt join is made up off the boat and the butt strap is too wide, you may have difficulty in getting the plywood planking to lie down on the frame work correctly so, as a guide I use 5" (125mm) wide ply straps for ¼" (6mm) plywood, 6" (150mm) wide straps for 3/8" (9mm) plywood and 8" (200mm) wide straps for ½" (12mm) plywood. I tend to use the same plywood for the strap as the plywood plank or slightly thicker.

On planking which consists of several layers, I still butt strap the inner layer (although some would argue that this is not necessary) and then stagger the butt joins on the remaining layers of plywood (Figure 59).

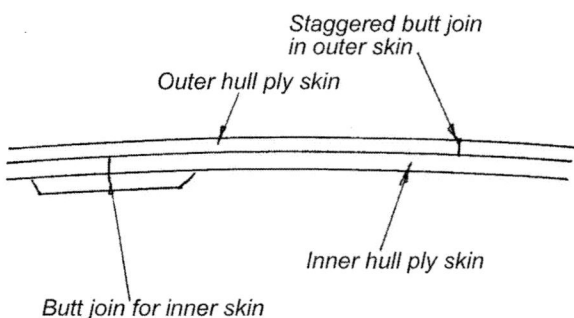

Fig 59. Staggering butt joins in a multi-layered hull skin.

I would consider scarfing the joins in the outer layer of plywood just to avoid any hard spots.

I do not like placing the butt joins over frames. Some builders do this in order to use the frame edge as a butt strap. I do not think that this gives sufficient glue area, for the butt to be a good join. I know placing the joins over the frames hides the join on the inside, but I don't think that this is a strong way to make the join – consequently I will move joins so that they occur between frames. Remember if you are making the join up 'off' the boat, allow for the chine stringers etc in the strap's shape.

I prefer to make the join over a substantial piece of scrap plywood that I can nail or screw into, to hold the plank pieces together whilst the glue cures. I first protect the scrap ply with PVC sheet so that the joining pieces of plywood do not get glued to it. Having cut and shaped the butt strap I then nail or screw this through the 2 pieces of plywood I am joining into the scrap plywood below so that nothing can move and to make sure that everything is nice and flat (Figure 60).

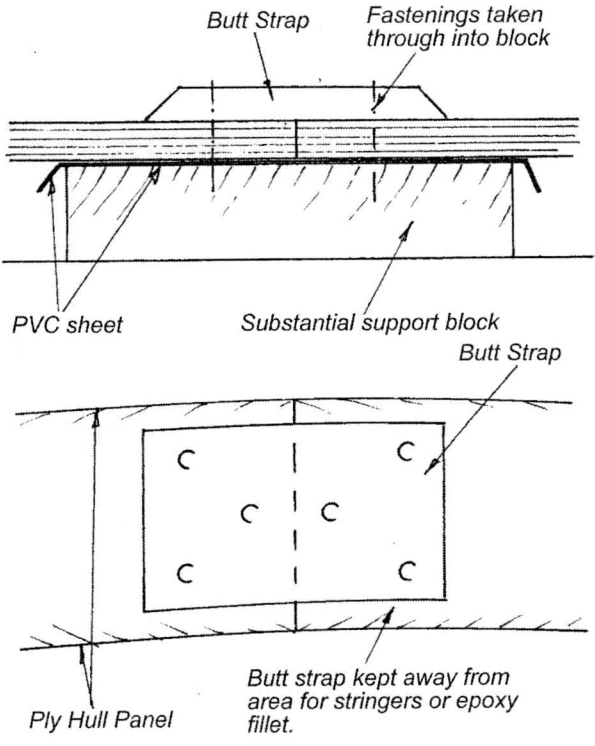

Fig 60. Assembling a butt join 'off' the framework.

6.2.2.2 Scarf Joins

The length of a scarf joint should be 6 to 8 times the thickness of the plank, so that for a 1/4" (6mm) plank, it should be around 2" (50mm) long (Figure 61).

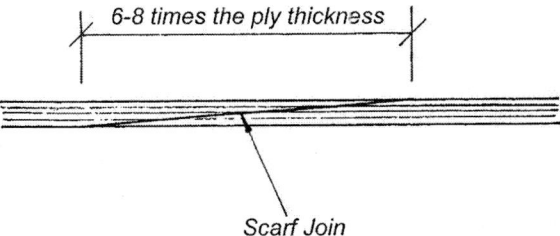

Fig 61. A scarf join in plywood.

With stitch and tape hulls where the plank shapes are pre-determined you will need to allow for the width of the scarf when marking the planks out. The best way to do this, is to mark out one part of the plank as normal, but then to start marking the mateing piece of plank the length of the scarf joint away from the edge of the ply sheet. The lines for the edge of the plank should be projected back over the scarf allowance (Figure 62).

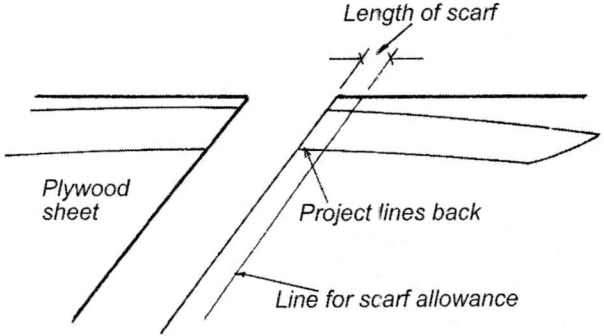

Fig 62. Allowing for the width of the scarf when marking out the plank/panel.

A good way to plane scarfs, is to do 2 or more at a time by clamping them to a bench top with the edge of the lower plank up to the edge of the bench and the next plank on top of the first, but with it's edge butting up to the inner scarf line of the lower plank (Figure 63). Plane carefully with a sharp, finely set plane, using the plywood laminates as a guide. These will show as straight lines across the ply, if the surface that you are planing is flat. Check that the surface is good and flat with a straight edge.

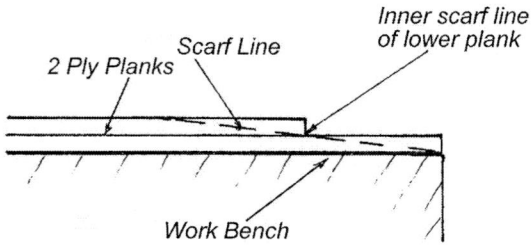

Fig 63. Planing a scarf on the work bench.

Above—using the veneers to guide when planning a scarf onto plywood.

When gluing the scarf joint, put pvc sheet down first, apply the glue liberally and use heavy staples to hold the ply together and to prevent it from slipping whilst you clamp it up. This is a slightly delicate operation and it is best to have some patient help around. The cramps should be applied over lengths of wood above and below the joint so that the clamping pressure is spread evenly across the width of the joint. Use pvc (plastic shopping bags) between the lengths of wood and the plank to prevent them from sticking to the

plank. Again, for multi-layered ply hull planking the scarf joints want to be staggered between the planks so that they are not adjacent to each other.

Once the glue has cured, the cramps can be removed and the edges of the plank planed up. For scarfed planks especially, you may need to check that the planks have been correctly aligned (do this before the glue has cured!) by running a line between the lower fore and aft points of the plank and checking the measurement from the line to the middle lower edge of the plank against the drawings (Figure 64).

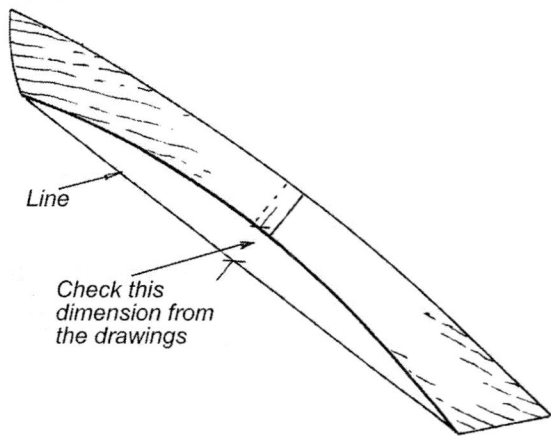

Fig 64. Checking the overall shape of a plank/ panel.

Some builders will cut and plane the scarf 'off' the boat and then assemble and glue the scarf 'on' the boat to make sure that the plank is the correct overall shape. This is a good compromise but leaves us with the difficulty of closing the scarf join properly between the top and bottom of the scarf. To do this I use a scrap PVC coated piece of wood on the inboard side of the join and screw though a similar piece of wood on the outboard side directly through the scarf to firmly clamp the pieces together – the screw holes are then filled later (Figure 65). Alternatively, arrange the scarfs to occur over the edge of a frame which will give you a good solid 'backing' to work against in closing the scarf.

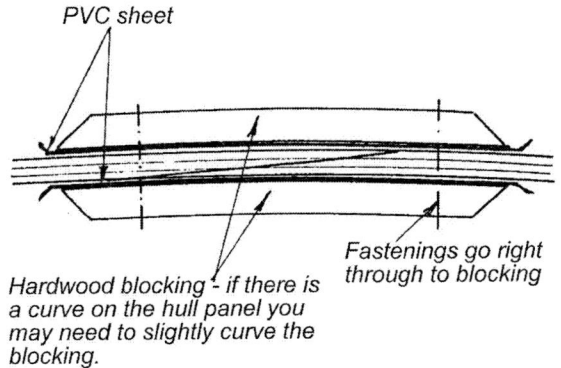

PVC sheet

Hardwood blocking - if there is a curve on the hull panel you may need to slightly curve the blocking.

Fastenings go right through to blocking

Fig 65. Clamping the scarf 'on' the boat.

6.2.3 Planking for Stitch and Tape Hulls

Once the framework is complete and prepared for planking, simply mark and cut out the plywood planks. The plywood plank shapes are rarely given full-size unless they are plotted onto expensive Mylar sheets – plotting onto ordinary paper is not very accurate as the paper will shrink and stretch and for larger boats with long panels/planks, this can be disastrous. On Selway Fisher Design plans we use a simple method of accurately marking out the plank/panel shapes directly onto the plywood sheets :-

A.   Look at the design sheet showing the hull panel/plank shapes and you will see a drawing showing one or more standard sheets of plywood laid edge to edge with the panel/plank shapes drawn on them and a series of parallel station lines drawn across the ply. These are usually spaced at 305mm (12") intervals. The dimensions for the panel/plank shapes are measured along these station lines – so the first job is to draw these station lines down onto the plywood – see Figure 66.

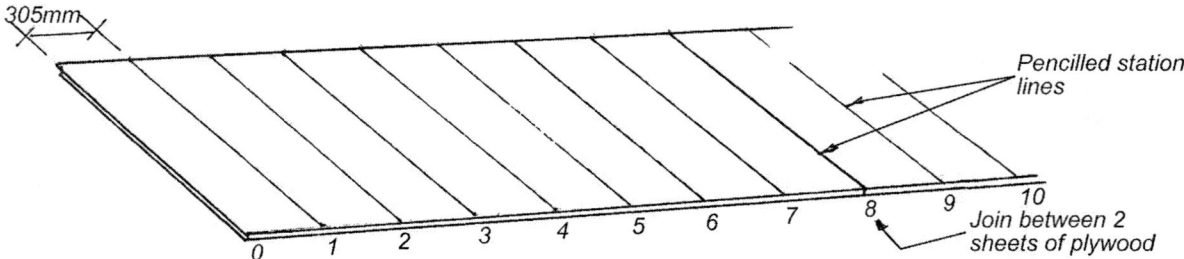

305mm

Pencilled station lines

0 1 2 3 4 5 6 7 8 9 10

Join between 2 sheets of plywood

Fig 66.

B.   Next, put your tape measure along each of these station lines in turn and mark off the dimensions given for the top and bottom (chine, gunwale lines etc) of each panel – Figure 67. Take your time and make sure you make a bold mark for each measurement – note that in most cases all the dimensions given are measured from the lower edge of the ply sheet.

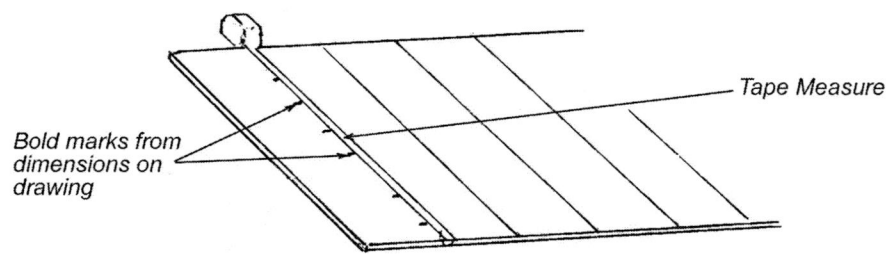

Bold marks from dimensions on drawing

Tape Measure

Fig 67.

C.   You can now mark the end points for each line – for instance, at the bow end of each panel the end points are defined by a distance up from the lower edge of the plywood sheet and horizontally from an adjacent station line – see Figure 68.

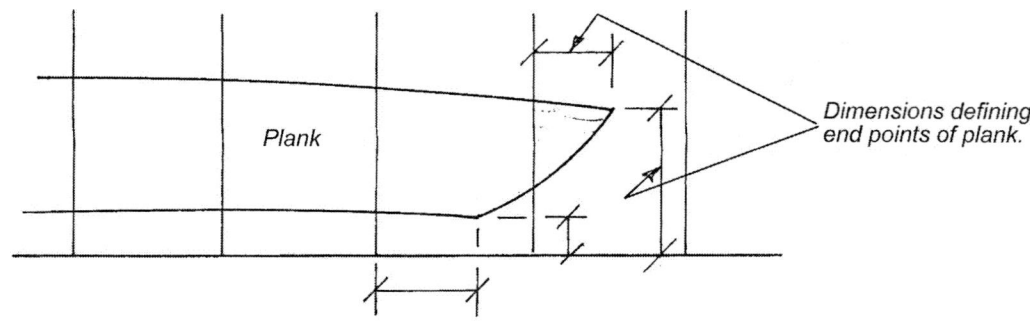

Plank

Dimensions defining end points of plank.

Fig 68.

D. Sometimes a particular curve (often a bow end curve), is defined by a series of squares – see Figure 69 – the size of the squares will be given – draw these onto the plywood sheet aligned as shown against a station line, and sketch in the curve using the squares as a guide.

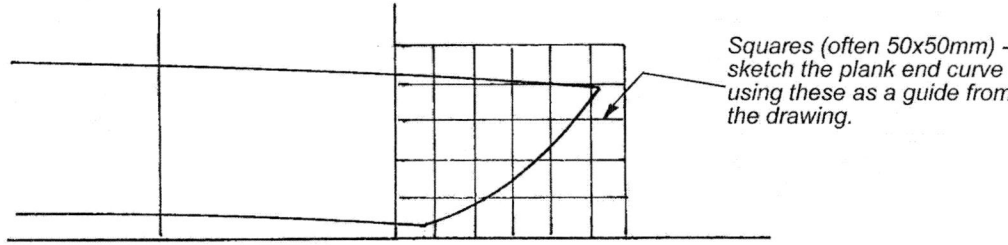

Squares (often 50x50mm) - sketch the plank end curve using these as a guide from the drawing.

Fig 69.

E. Now we can draw in the long curves defining the panels/planks – do this using a long thin batten (a piece of old plastic curtain rail or thin plastic wiring conduit which you can obtain from a DIY store, is excellent for this) – hold the batten down with weights or nails to pass through each mark on the station lines and draw in each curve with a bold pencil line – see Figure 70

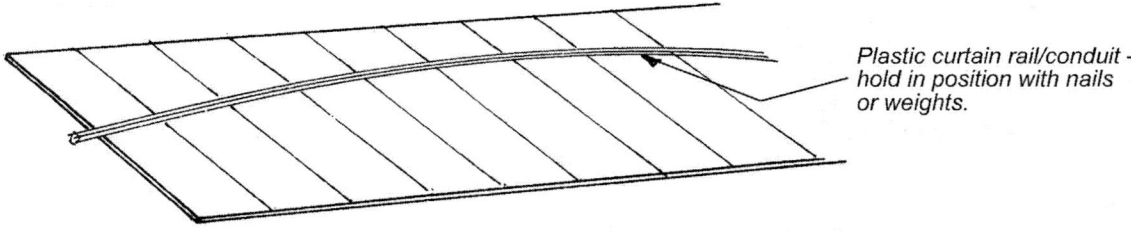

Plastic curtain rail/conduit - hold in position with nails or weights.

Fig 70.

F. Mark any frame positions given on the drawings onto the hull panels/planks.

G. Now you can cut out the panel/plank shapes – I use a single speed jig saw with a fine blade holding the ply sheet on a workmate/saw horse – cut approximately 1mm from the line. You can either mark out each panel separately (port and starboard) or mark and cut out one set of panels (say the port side) and use these as templates for the other set (starboard side).

H.   Once all the panels have been cut out, you can use your workmate (bench vice etc) to hold each individual pair of panels together so that they can be planed up carefully (to the line) together.

Having prepared the planks, carefully 'drape' them over the framework – use as few fastenings as possible to start with until you have made any adjustments necessary to get them into the correct position – in particular, do not fasten the planking into 2 adjacent frames until you have bent the plank/panel over the whole hull or you may end up with 'flat' areas between the frames (Figure 71).

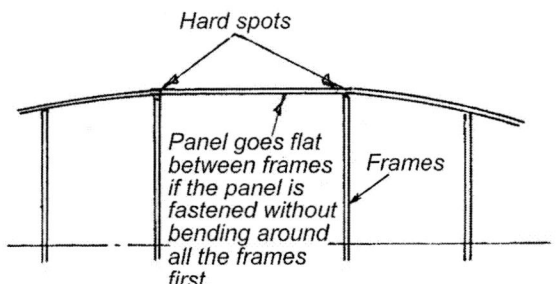

Fig 71.

Having dry screwed or stitched the plank shapes in place and made adjustments, you can then remove the planks/panels and refit with any epoxy required between the edges of the frames and the inside surface of the hull plank/panel.

6.2.4 For Plywood Plank Over Frame Hulls

For designs where the builder does not have the stitch and tape plank/panel shapes, the framework has to have chine stringers etc in order to define the shape of the hull planks/panels – so we are starting with a full framework rather than just interlocking plywood frames and girders as we might have for the stitch and tape boat. Consequently, planking done this way is a matter of putting the rough plywood plank/panel shapes onto the framework and trimming back for their correct shape after they have been fixed into place.

This all sounds quite simple but, there is a sensible way to do it which avoids potential problems. We also have to make choices over how we finish the plywood planks/panels at the chines etc and there may be problems in trimming to a 'true' chine line where adjacent planks meet each other almost 'end-on' (usually towards the bow).

Let's start with the simple part of the planking process first. This covers most of the hull area. We normally start by planking at the garboard (lowest plank on the hull adjacent to the centreline/keel structure). If the hull is not too big and the planking not too thick and therefore heavy, you can simply manoeuvre a sheet of ply up to and over the area to be planked, hold it temporarily in place, go inside the hull framework and mark round the ply to get the rough shape required (Figure 72).

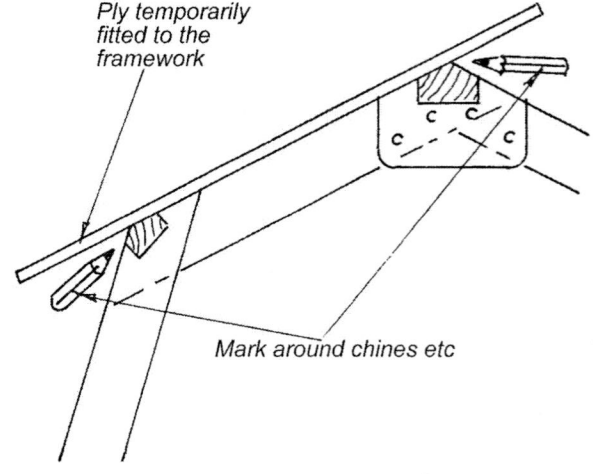

Fig 72.

The position of the ply sheet can then be marked onto the framework and be removed, cut and the piece of ply offered back up to the hull to make any final adjustments before it is glued and fastened into place. If the plywood is too heavy to do this easily then use hardboard sheets which are much lighter to take 'templates' off the framework which can then be transferred to the plywood. Some builders, especially on larger plywood boats, prefer to take a template off the frame for large areas of the plywood planking/paneling – this enables them to scarf up plywood to cover large areas of the hull planking/paneling off the boat (Figure 73).

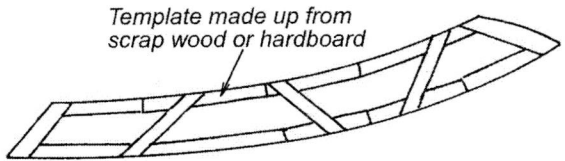

Template made up from scrap wood or hardboard

Fig 73.

At the centreline some builders prefer to cut the plywood roughly to shape and then to 'spile' the plank/panel shape using a spiling block (Figure 74).

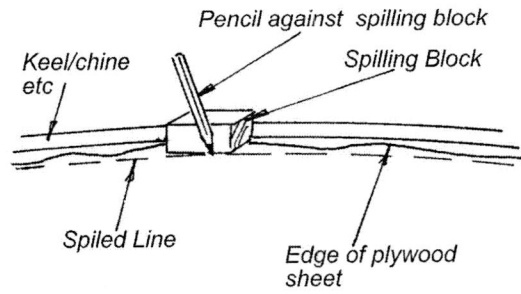

Pencil against spilling block
Spilling Block
Keel/chine etc
Spiled Line
Edge of plywood sheet

Fig 74.

At one time, when glues and resins were not as efficient as they are today, it was considered essential in professional plywood boat construction, to use a hardwood edging to the plywood planks/panels – this edging was often part of the chine stringer (Figure 75).

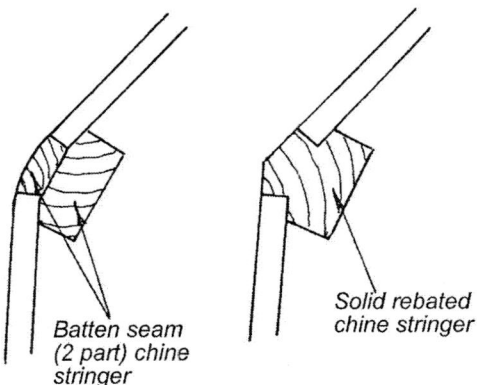

Batten seam (2 part) chine stringer
Solid rebated chine stringer

Fig 75.

With modern glues and resins, it is much more acceptable to simply overlap the hull planks/panels and fill the end grain of the exposed edge of the ply with thickened epoxy (Figure 76). This is fine for smaller boats (less than 18' (5.5m).

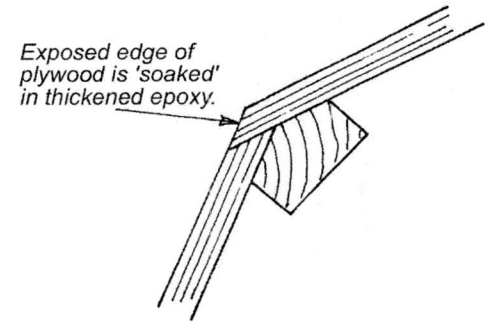

Exposed edge of plywood is 'soaked' in thickened epoxy.

Fig 76.

For larger boats, the exposed edges of the plywood must still be treated so that they do not absorb moisture and the way to do this is to use several coats of epoxy resin and then to sheath the hull. If the hull is not to be sheathed overall, then some builders route back over the outside ply skins a width and depth to allow a glass tape in epoxy resin to lie flush with the plywood (Figure 77).

59

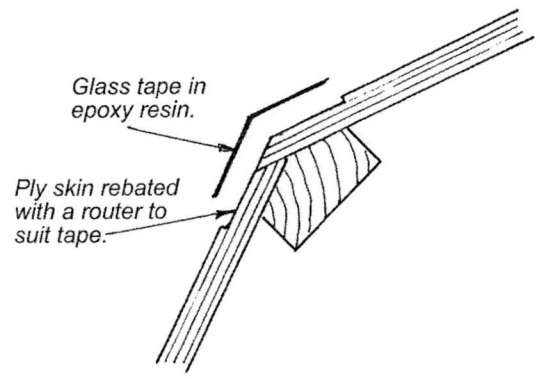

Glass tape in epoxy resin.

Ply skin rebated with a router to suit tape.

Fig 77.

So far, we have looked at the application of the hull planks/panels for simple chines with a good angle between the hull panels – but what happens at the bow of the boat where the planks/panels meet each other at the chines almost edge to edge? As the chines progress towards the bow, the angle between the hull planks/panels becomes more and more 'open' or 'obtuse' until you get to the point where it almost impossible to bevel any material off to make the planks lie properly together (Figure 78).

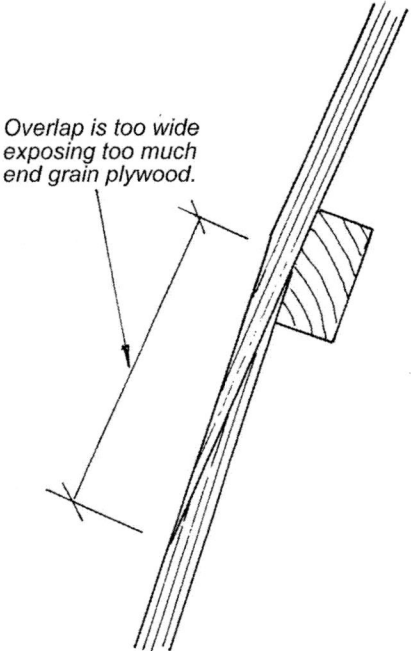

Overlap is too wide exposing too much end grain plywood.

Fig 78. The difficulty of using a simple overlap where the angle between the panels is very obtuse

The sensible way to overcome this problem is to change from simply chamfering the hull plank/panel to accept it's adjacent plank/panel and bring them together edge to edge – this means cutting a step in the plywood – Figure 79).

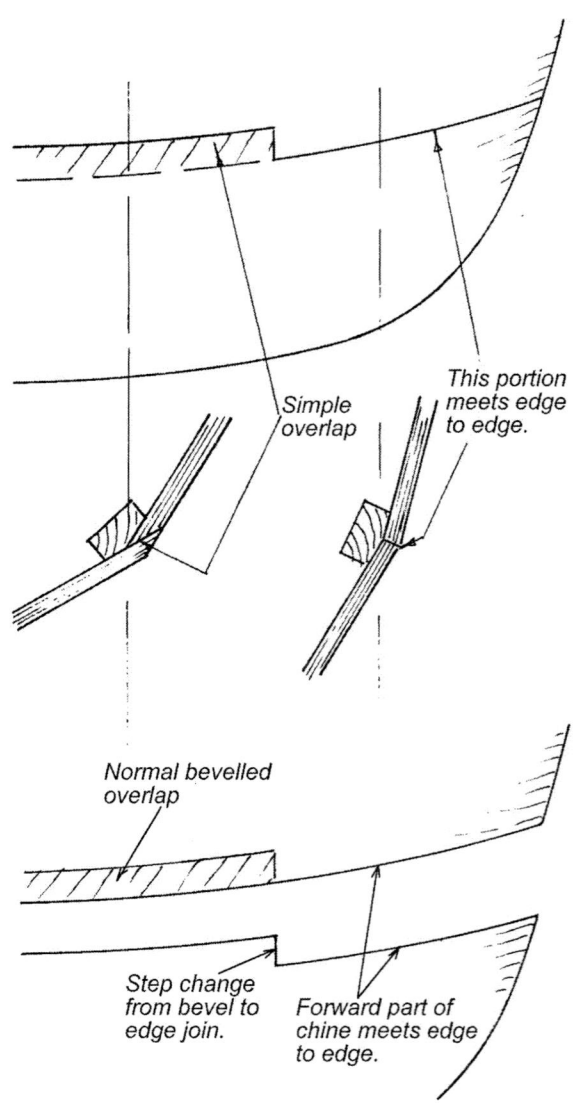

Simple overlap

This portion meets edge to edge.

Normal bevelled overlap

Step change from bevel to edge join.

Forward part of chine meets edge to edge.

Fig 79. The step change in chines often used towards the bow between a simple overlap and edge to edge meeting of the hull panels.

6.3 Finishing a Plywood Hull

Once all the plywood planking/panelling is in place we then need to choose how we are going to finish it. Rather than just going for a paint finish on a larger ply hull, my preference is to sheath the hull in glass and epoxy. This gives the hull a hard outer surface which will greatly protect the plywood hull skin and give a very hard surface onto which paint can be applied. For larger trailer-able boats the sheathing will protect against the inevitable knocks and scrapes that the hull will receive and for a boat left on a mooring, the sheathing will protect against floating debris. The reason we need to discuss this now is because if we are going to sheath, this should be done with the hull upside down and before keels, skegs and rubbing strakes or bilge keels are fitted.

6.3.1 Painting Only

If you decide to go for a paint finish without sheathing then now is also the time to do some surface preparation and some initial painting, before the hull is turned over – it is much easier to work down onto an upturned hull than it is to work underneath an upright hull. If you are going to paint only, the first task after sanding, fairing and filling all the screw heads etc is to mask off any areas that you do not want painted – ie., areas which are still to take glue. When this is complete, you can start with a good quality primer and under coat system, doing as much painting as is sensible before you turn the hull over. For a painted only hull, you may have already fitted the skeg and keel etc before you paint but in some cases this is not done because turning the hull over may be easier before the keel/skeg is finally bolted into place. See Chapter 10 for a fuller explanation of the painting process.

6.3.2 Sheathing

Always sheath over a bare upside down hull. The gunwale rubbers, any skegs, deadwood or keel should not have been fitted and you may even choose not to fit the outer wood stem at this stage, leaving the hardwood outer stem to go on over the sheathing so that it can be easily replaced should it ever get damaged. Surfaces which are to accept outer stems, keels and skegs later should be planned flat and wide enough to accept the item later.

Preparation is all important - there should be no sharp or 'quick' changes in shape and if there are any, these should be filled out with epoxy fillers so that the glass cloth used for the sheathing will lie over them without difficulty. Very 'sharp' chines and transom corners should be rounded for the same reason (Figure 80). All screw heads and any holes must be carefully filled with thickened epoxy and sanded flush with the ply skin.

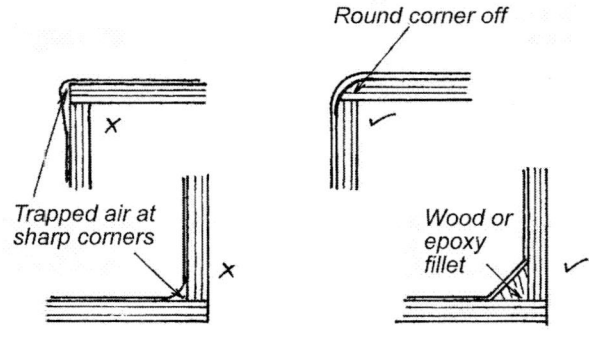

Fig 80. Avoiding sharp corners when sheathing.

Do not sheath early in the morning but wait for the day's temperature to stabilize. If you do not do this, it is quite likely that air trapped in the wood surface with expand later and 'out-gas' causing air to be trapped in the coating or sheathing.

There are 2 basic methods to sheath – the 'dry' and the 'wet' method. In both cases, the plywood hull should be given a coat of epoxy resin/hardener and allowed to cure. This should then be given a light sanding if necessary to 'flatten' any raised wood fibres before sheathing commences.

The 'wet' method involves painting or rolling on more epoxy over the hull surface and then applying the woven cloth rolling out any air bubbles and creases as you go. You can set yourself up by pinning the cloth to the centreline of the boat to hang down in 'drapes' each one overlapping it's neighbour by around 40 to 50 mm – roll the cloths back up out of the way, apply the resin in a fairly heavy coat to the ply surface and then roll each cloth in turn down over the wet area with a squeegee or split washer roller. However, in my experience, unless you have plenty of man-power who can do the rolling quickly before the epoxy starts to cure in a continuous process, this method is best left to the professionals – it can lead to panic as the epoxy starts to cure quicker than you hoped and before all the wrinkles are out of the cloth.

The 'dry' method involves working resin through the dry cloth as it lies on the dry hull surface. Prepare the sheathing by covering the hull with dry woven glass cloth and cutting it over length to suit with each cloth over lapping it's neighbours by 40-50 mm (Figure 81). The cloths are then removed and laid close to the job and in a sequence which allows you to put them back on again correctly. Take the first cloth, lay it in place and hold it with tacks or tape and then, starting from the middle of the cloth, work resin into the cloth with brush and roller working any air trapped underneath the cloth out towards the edges. Once the first cloth is coated in resin and wetted out, the next cloth

can then be put in place and the process repeated.

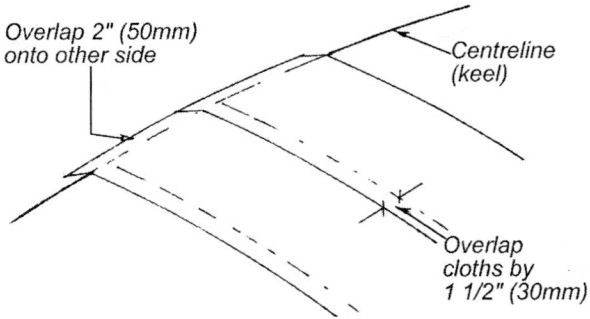

Fig 81. Laying the cloths over the hull for sheathing.

The cloth will go transparent as it wets out – any dry spots can have more resin applied to them to ensure that they are fully wetted out. I find that this 'dry' method of sheathing allows you to work single handed and at your own pace

If the sheathing has to go around compound shapes and corners, lift the cloth whilst it is still wet, cut it or slit it with a pair of scissors and brush into place allowing the cloth to overlap as necessary (Figure 82).

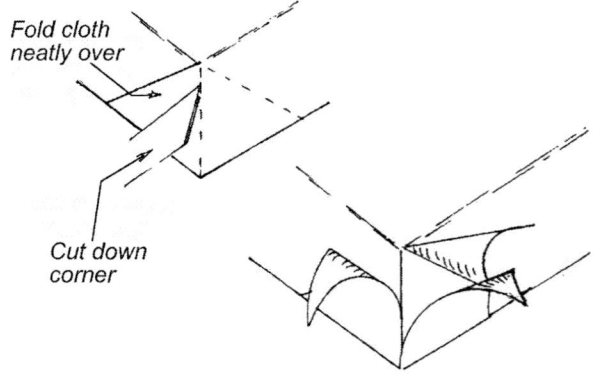

Fig 82. Sheathing around awkward shapes.

The design will specify what weight of cloth to use and how many layers of cloth to use. To simply protect the surface of the plywood on boats over 20' (6.1m) I usually use one or more layers of 300 gm woven roving but there are many different types of cloth and different weights. If a second layer of cloth is to be applied, wait for the first layer to cure and then repeat the process but do not wait too long after the first layer has cured or a good bond will not occur.

Overlapping the cloths is the strongest way to apply the sheathing and the bumps which occur can be filled with thickened epoxy fairing later. However, if an overlap is not required, wait for the epoxy to 'initially' cure, take a straight edge, lay it mid way over the lap and cut through with a sharp knife. Lift the excess piece of cloth off the top layer, lift the top layer over the under layer and remove the excess piece underneath and then roll the surfaces down again (Figure 83). Coat the

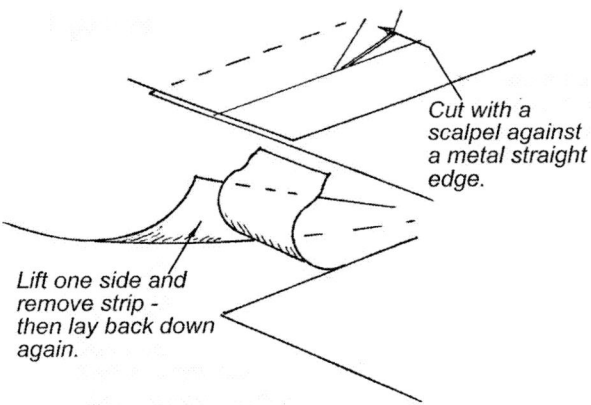

Cut with a scalpel against a metal straight edge.

Lift one side and remove strip - then lay back down again.

Fig 83. Removing the overlap.

surface of the final glass cloth with more resin before it has reached the final cure stage allow this to almost finally cure before applying more resin, repeating the process until the weave is filled.

Surface finishing and preparation for the application of paints and varnishes over the sheathing needs to be done carefully and most epoxy manufacturers have their own literature on this which you should be guided

by. I find however, that surface grinding and sanding prior to final finishing does not go well unless the epoxy already applied is fully cured. If the epoxy is not fully cured, sand paper gets easily clogged and paints and varnishes refuse to cure – so take your time and carefully follow manufacturers' instructions.

6.4 Clinker or Lapstrake Planking

Whilst this manual is really about 'multi-chine' boats where the plywood skin meets at the chines to form a 'corner', there is no reason why the same framework used for multi-chine construction cannot also be used for a clinker or lapstrake hull where the planks overlap each other at the 'chine' points.

There are one or two points that the builder needs to grasp when looking at clinker planking. This type of construction is usually considered to be the hardest form of boat building method you can use. The overlap between one plank and another varies both in width and in angle and needs to be worked with some care. The planks are usually 'let' into each other as they approach the bow so that at the stem itself, the planks are no longer 'stepped' or lapped but are flush with each other. If the overlap is carried right through to the stem, the stem would be ugly and any stem cap (outer stem) would have to be 'saw tooth' in shape to cover the ends of the stepped planks.

It would be virtually impossible to allow the planks to be stepped or lapped at the bow if the planks went into a traditionally rabbeted stem.

This all sounds daunting but the big advantage over traditional clinker/lapstrake construction that we have, is the framework.

Traditional clinker/lapstrake construction used virtually no framework at all and just a few 'moulds' (sectional shapes) erected upside down. These moulds were often round in shape and not even stepped (or cornered) to show where the planks overlapped. It was the job of the builder to decide how many planks he/she was going to use and where the laps occurred and then to take ('spile') the planks shapes from the moulds.

The framework that we have already built for a multi-chine hull, with it's chine stringers, means that we already have a framework that easily allows us to 'spile' the shapes of the clinker planks.

The garboard plank (first plank against the hog/centerline) is the same shape as the garboard plank/panel used in multi-chine construction. The next plank is also the same as that on the multi-chine boat but instead of the lower edge being trimmed and planed down to a ridge, it is left 'proud' to form the clinker lap. Figure 84 shows the process for the Selway Fisher 22' Rona yacht which can be built using either the multi-chine stitch and tape process or the clinker ply process.

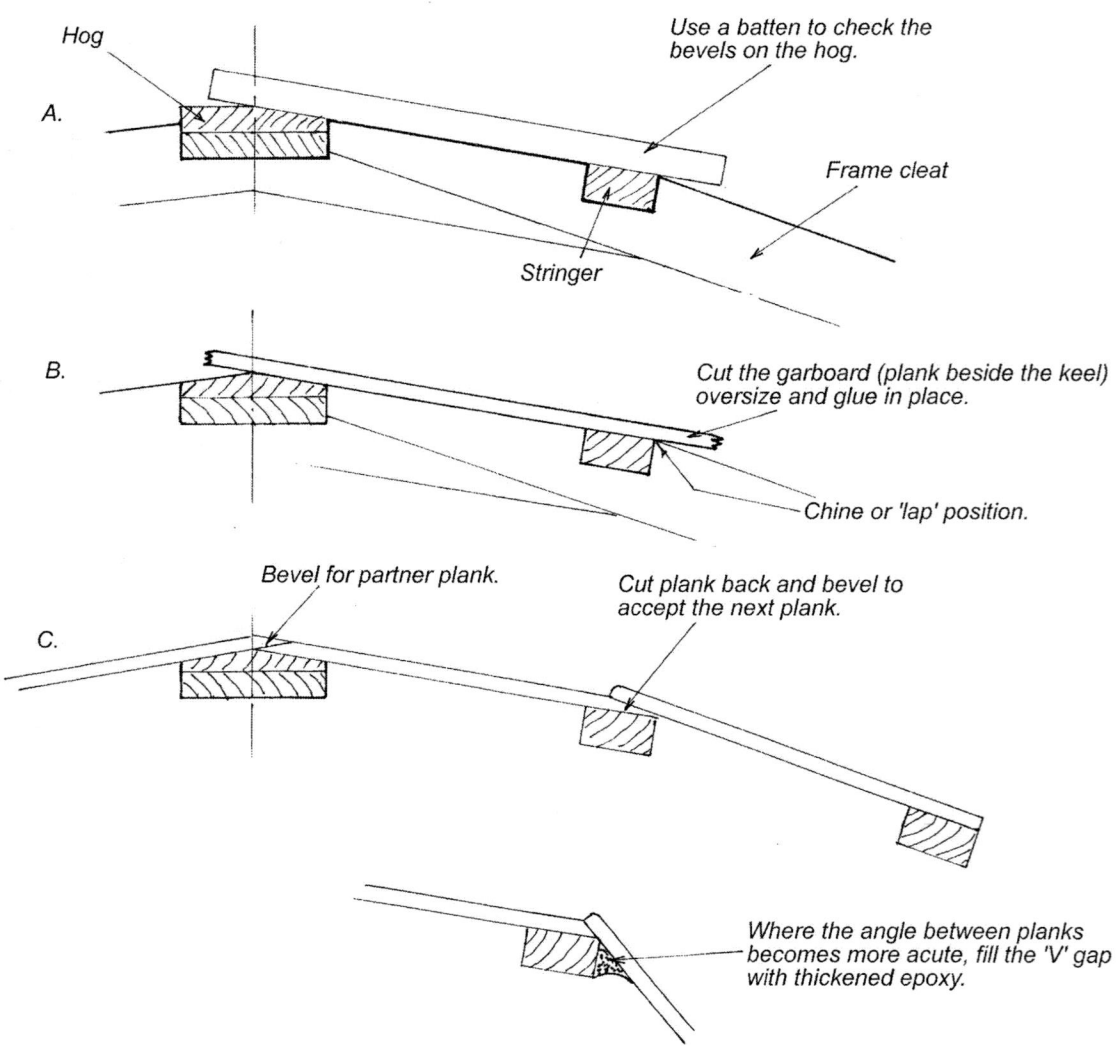

Fig 84.

At the bow (and stern of double ended yachts) and often, at the transom, the planks have to be 'let' into each other so that when they arrive at the bow or transom, they are not stepped over each other as they are in the remainder of the hull. If you look at Figure 84 you will see how the planks end up 'stepped' or 'lapped' over each other which is the whole point of the clinker building method—but if we allow these same 'steps' or 'laps' to continue right to the bow, the outer shape of the stem will need to have a 'saw-tooth' shape each side to accommodate these 'laps'. This, as we have already mentioned, is both difficult to do and very ugly. So, as the planks approach the bow they are 'let' into each other in such a way that they arrive at the bow 'flush' with each other (Figure 85).

As the planks approach the stem and transom 'let' the planks into each other so that they become 'flush' with each other.

Note - this illustration shows the planks part way along the transition from being overlapped to being 'flush' at the bow.

Fig 85.

The process of cutting these tapered 'lets' or 'gains' requires skill with chisels and rebate planes but is not beyond most relatively competent woodworkers. Apart from the skills, the process requires three things—

sharp tools, patience (in continuously offering up the plank to be fitted to the plank having the 'let' or 'gain' cut in it) and high quality materials. Making a clinker/lapstrake hull with anything other than high quality multi-laminate marine plywood (with laminates of equal thickness and not the thick bulk core type plywood), is frustrating and ultimately disastrous, from the point of view of gaining a crisp, clean finish.

Above— a Selway Fisher Suffolk Beach Punt built by Mr. Ian Gardner showing the clinker planks 'let' into each other as they approach the stem. The line of the outer stem against the ends of the planks shows that they are completely 'flush' with each other at the point.

As the planks approach the transom the planks need to go through a similar process except that where the angle between adjacent planks is reasonable and not so obtuse (wide), the planks can be 'lapped'. However, where the angle between the planks becomes too obtuse (usually below the turn of the bilge), the planks need to be 'let' into each other (Figure 87). A good example of this is shown on the photograph of the stern of the 'Kane' Suffolk Beach Punt built by Mr. Ian Gardner on Page 68.

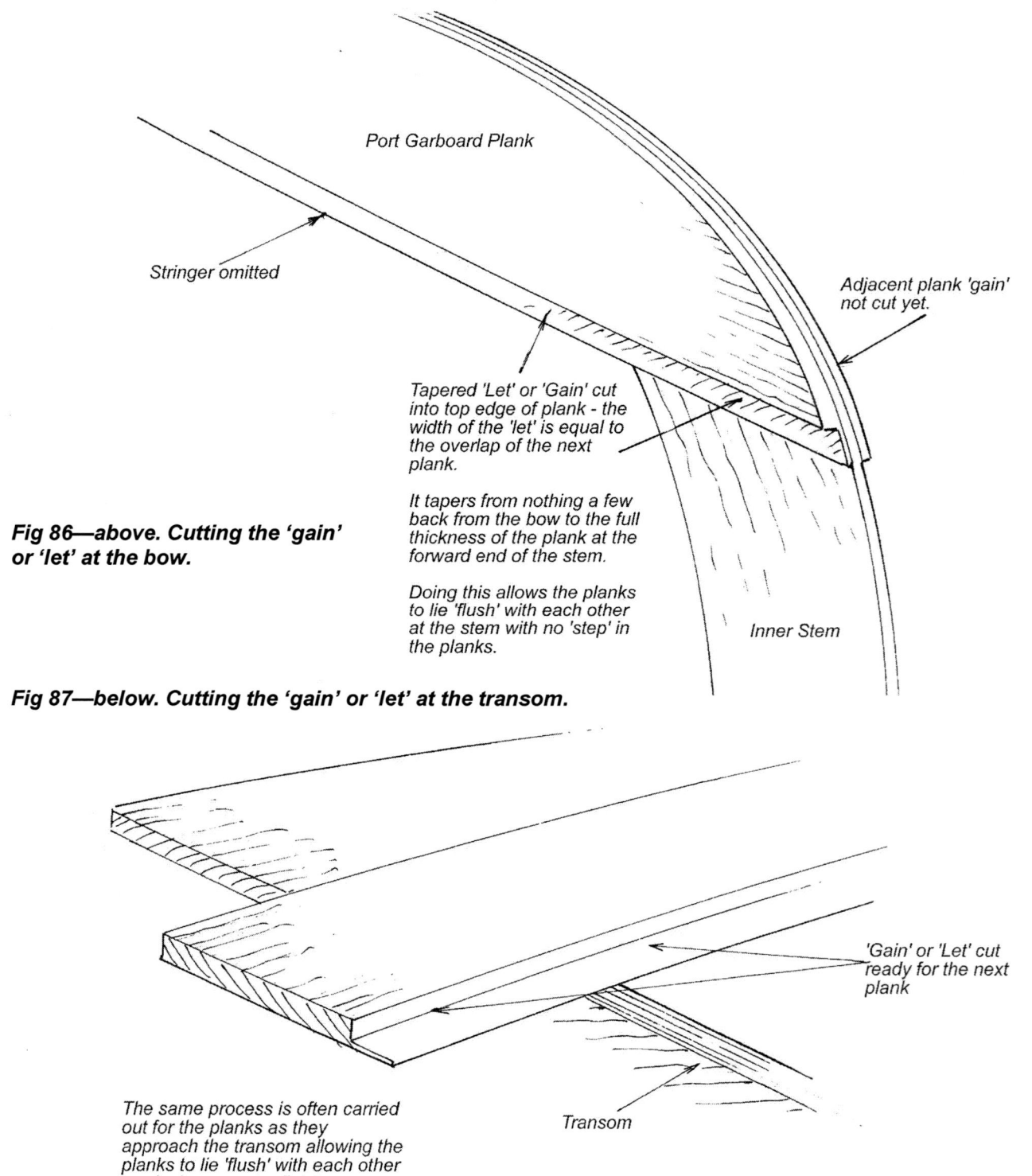

Port Garboard Plank

Stringer omitted

Adjacent plank 'gain' not cut yet.

Tapered 'Let' or 'Gain' cut into top edge of plank - the width of the 'let' is equal to the overlap of the next plank.

It tapers from nothing a few back from the bow to the full thickness of the plank at the forward end of the stem.

Doing this allows the planks to lie 'flush' with each other at the stem with no 'step' in the planks.

Fig 86—above. Cutting the 'gain' or 'let' at the bow.

Inner Stem

Fig 87—below. Cutting the 'gain' or 'let' at the transom.

'Gain' or 'Let' cut ready for the next plank

Transom

The same process is often carried out for the planks as they approach the transom allowing the planks to lie 'flush' with each other producing a neater finish.

Often along the topsides in the middle of the boat, the plank angle is again very obtuse. In this area, an overlap is usually still required otherwise the planking does not look correct and this leaves a gap between the frame/ and cleat and the inside of the planking. Therefore the frames need to be 'packed' and filled to take up the gap (Figure 88).

Although not shown here, the amount that one plank overlaps another (known as the 'lap' or 'hemming' width) is usually at least twice the thickness of the planking—so 12mm planking would have a 'lap' width of at least 24mm. If you think about it, the stringers are set up to give fair plank shapes and therefore, in bevelling a plank to accept

it's adjacent plank, we do not normally want to deviate from a constant 'lap' width along the length of the plank—otherwise, the line of the plank laps will deviate from the line of the plank set up by the stringers. This 'lap' width is often drawn onto the top edge of a plank and the bevel taken to this 'hemming' line and not allowed to deviate across it—this leads to the need for frames to be well packed as already mentioned. *Note, for a fuller explanation of the Clinker Planking process, see the Selway Fisher Manual of Clinker Plywood Boat Construction Techniques.*

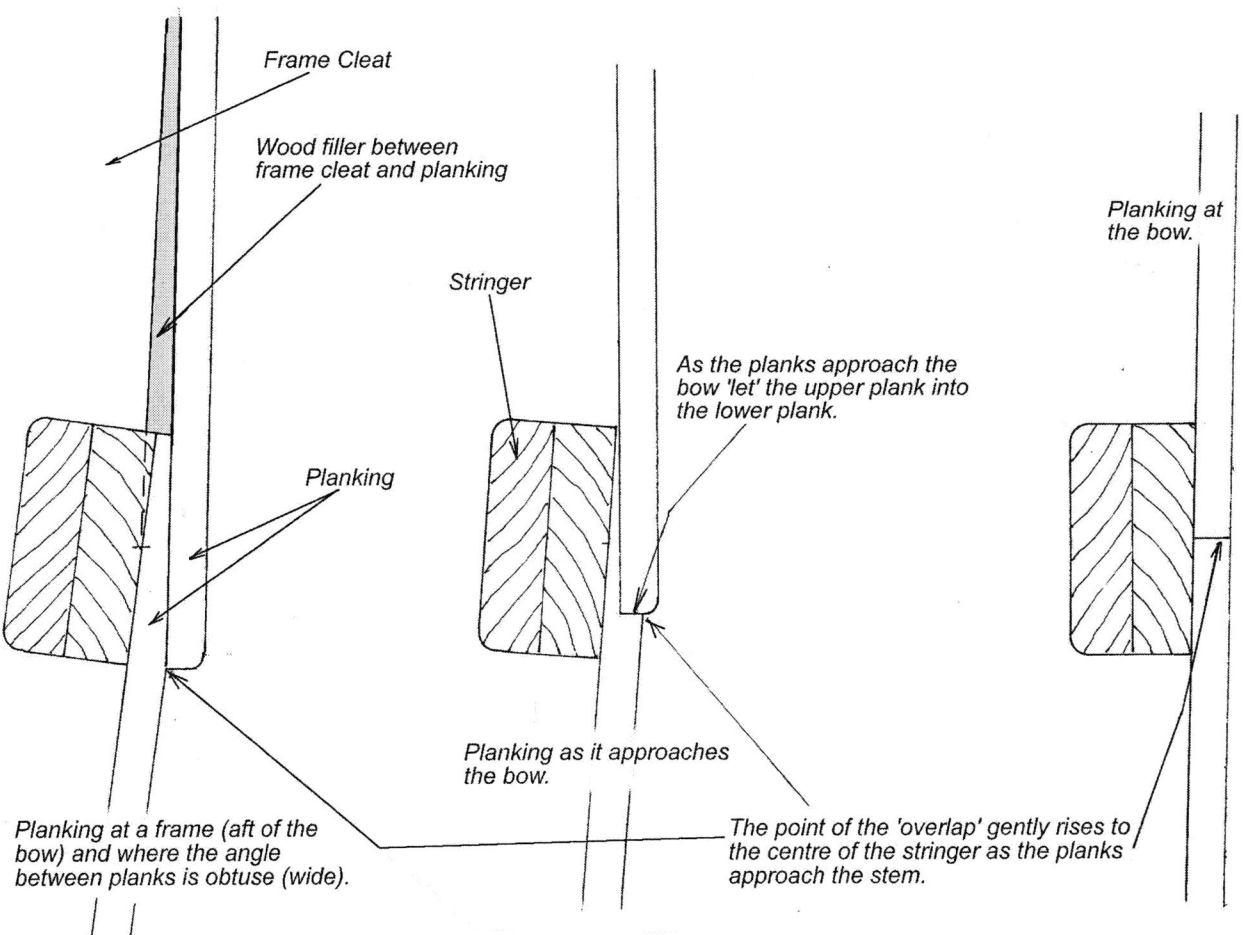

Fig 88. This diagram is from the plans of the 30' Martlet gaff cutter showing that where there is an obtuse angle between the planks, the frames need a filler piece (left). The change in 'lap' is also shown as it approaches the bow (right).

Above— The clinker planks as they approach the transom—the upper planks are 'lapped' but the lower planks have 'gains/lets' cut into them.

Chapter 7

THE HULL EXTERIOR
KEELS, SKEGS, MARKING THE WATERLINE, TURNING OVER

7.1 Fitting Gunwale Rubbers etc.

If gunwale rubbers etc are to be replaceable then they can be applied with a layer of mastic (ie., One part 'Life-Caulk' etc) and screwed into place. If they are not designed to be removed then they can be fitted with thickened epoxy and screwed or bolted into place (Figure 89). Note how the lower rubber is fitted to the ply hull skin only and therefore is screwed into from the plywood side—do not try and hold any item onto plywood by screwing through the item and into the plywood—it will rarely hold unless the plywood is massively thick.

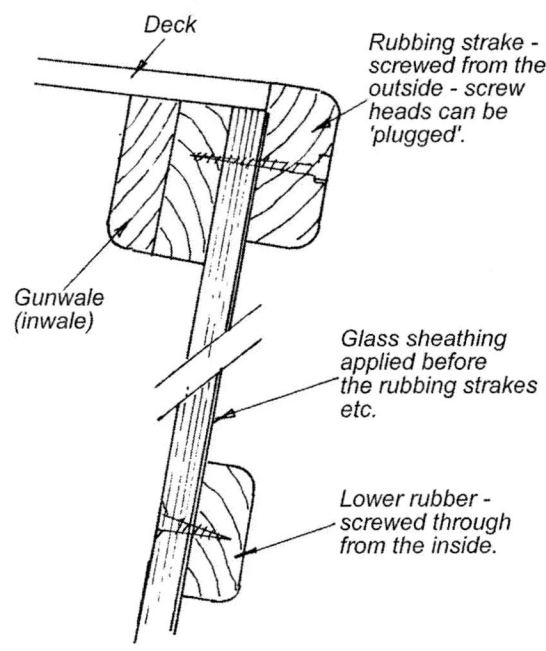

Deck

Rubbing strake - screwed from the outside - screw heads can be 'plugged'.

Gunwale (inwale)

Glass sheathing applied before the rubbing strakes etc.

Lower rubber - screwed through from the inside.

Fig 89. Fitting the rubbing strakes.

69

7.2 Skegs, Deadwood and Wood Keels

This section covers simple skegs, exterior stems etc and does not touch on ballast keels, fitting sterngear (shafts and stern tubes) or rudders—the construction and fitting of these items is covered in the Selway Fisher Manual of Boat Fit-Out for Yachts and Motor Cruisers.

If the hull has been built upside down, first consider whether you want to fit the skeg/deadwood permanently before turning the hull upright – bilge keels and central keels can make turning the boat over more difficult and sometimes it is better the make up, shape and fit these items 'dry' before turning the hull over, remove them and finally refit, with the hull upright.

For keel/deadwood and skegs I take a pattern off the hull using scrap wood or hardboard. I shape the edge of the hardboard or scrap wood to exactly fit the area of hull to which the skeg or deadwood/keel is going to be fitted (Figure 90).

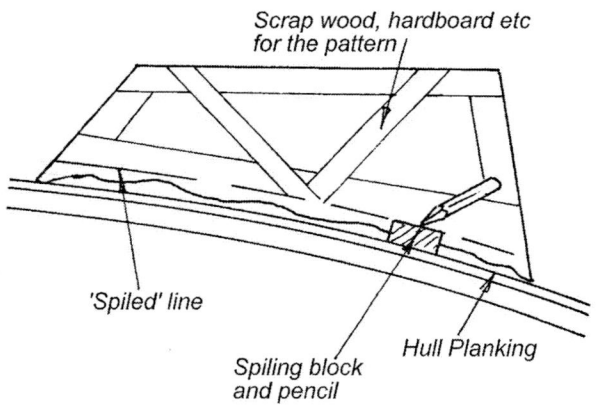

Fig 90. 'Spiling' the shape of the deadwood/skeg off the hull.

I then hold the hardboard in place and, using the Reference/Datum line to take vertical measurements from, draw on the outer shape of the skeg/keel etc. This is then cut to shape and offered back up to the hull for a final check. Any stern-tube or shaft line can be drawn on at the same time. This pattern is then used 'off' the boat to help laminate up the necessary wood or fabricate any steel plate keel etc.

The real item can then be offered up to the hull and taken off for any adjustments to be made before being finally shaped with any tapers etc. Holes for fixing bolts can be drilled and the whole item dry bolted in place.

7.2.1 Fitting Skegs/Deadwood

Figure 91 shows a simple arrangement for a wood skeg on a plywood cruiser. This consists of a wood triangular shaped skeg/deadwood deeper at it's aft end to protect the leg of the outboard or the propeller of an inboard engine. The skeg tapers in it's profile shape towards the bow where it finally blends into the outer stem.

Rather than trying to make up the skeg from one solid piece of wood, it is made up from several horizontal 'lifts' which are glued and bolted together. A solid bottom piece is used to cover the end grain of the horizontal pieces and it is this piece which blends into the outer stem at it's forward end.

To cover the end grain of the 'lifts' at their aft end, a vertical piece may be used which is part 'checked' into the bottom skeg piece.

If the skeg/deadwood is to be bolted it is best to use full length bolts with their bottom ends 'pocketed' into the bottom skeg piece.

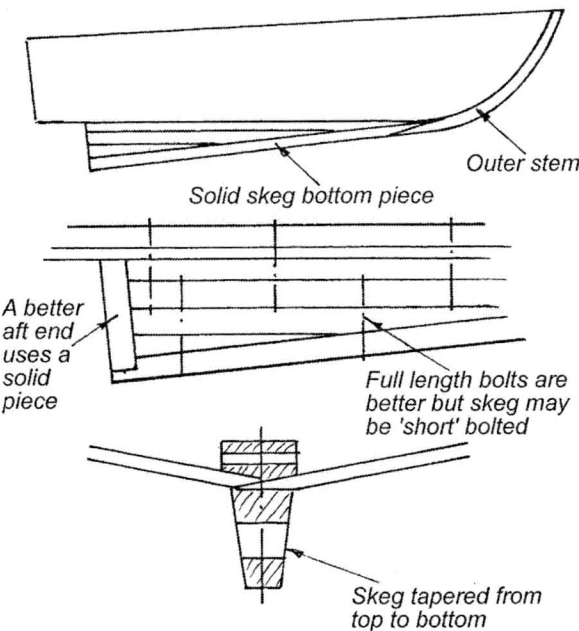

Fig 91. A typical simple triangular skeg/ deadwood used on a plywood motor cruiser.

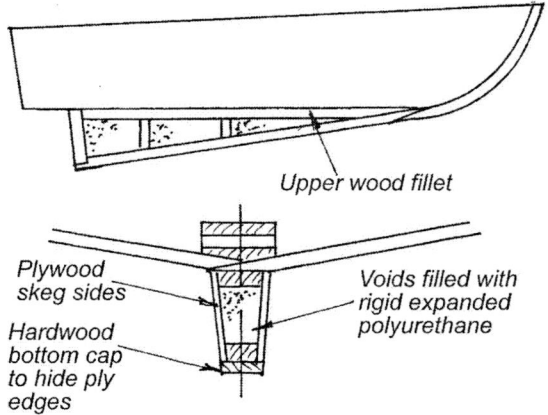

Fig 92. A hollow skeg.

However, full length bolts can be difficult to obtain or are expensive and therefore 1 sometimes use 'short' bolting' - shorter bolts used between the 'lifts' and staggered so that the skeg is adequately fastened.

It is a good idea to use large washers under the bolt heads even though there may not be a lot of stress on the keel—and use large washers under the nuts too. Notice in the section of the skeg shown in Figure 91 that the skeg is usually tapered in section from top to bottom—how much, is usually specified on the drawings. The bottom of the skeg and outer face of the outer stem may also have a bronze or stainless steel covering plate to further protect it.

Figure 92 shows a similar shaped skeg but hollow. The advantage of this type of skeg is that it is cheaper to make and often allows you to use scrap and offcuts of plywood to make it up.

It is important that all the edges of the plywood sides are covered and protected with hardwood and the inside is often filled with Rigid Expanded Polyurethane Foam—the box is made up and dry fixed to the upper wood fillet. It is then removed, filled with the foam and then refitted with glue.

This type of skeg is often sheathed in glass/epoxy separately from the hull—the join between the side of the skeg box and the hull is then covered by a large epoxy fillet.

Where the solid skeg bottom piece joins the outer stem there needs to be a strong and well cut join. This is usually a scarf join (a lipped or hooked scarf is best) with it's slope running aft to protect the skeg should the boat hit something under the water—Figure 93.

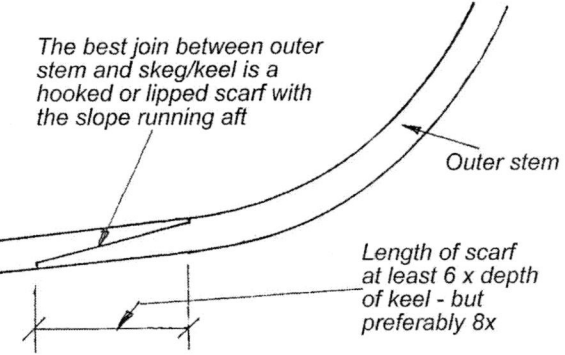

Fig 93. The stem/skeg join.

7.2.2 The Outer Stem

If we assume that the bow is curved in profile, then the outer stem is usually laminated rather than made up from solid wood pieces. The ends of the plywood planking need to be planed first, to give a 'flat' area wide enough to take the outer stem. The hull is then usually sheathed at this point before the outer stem, skeg etc is fitted—Figure 94.

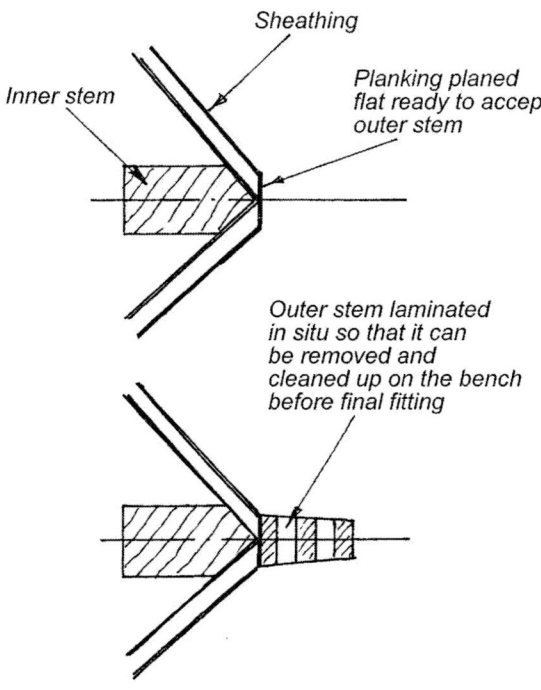

Fig 94. Preparing the hull for the outer stem.

It is difficult to properly clean up and taper the sides of the outer stem when it is fastened to the hull and so 1 prefer to laminate it in such a way that it can removed and taken to the bench so that it can be finally shaped before final fitting. To do this cover the hull in way of the outer stem with PVC so that glue squeezing from the laminates does not glue the outer stem prematurely to the hull.

To hold the laminates in place 1 sometimes use timber and wedges braced against the roof of the building shed or dry screw the laminates at their extreme ends so that the screws can be easily removed. Alternatively, you can use screws just long enough to fasten into the adjacent laminates without going right through into the hull.

Once cleaned up, the outer stem can then be refitted with epoxy, to the hull and finally fastened though to the inner stem—Figure 95.

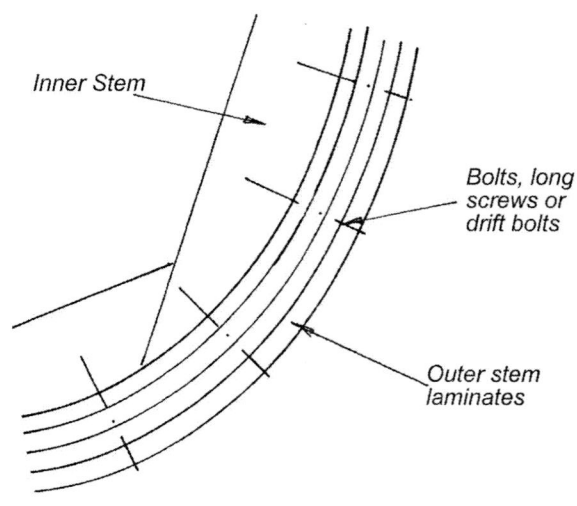

Fig 95. Finally fitting the outer stem to the hull.

7.2.3 Bilge Runners

Often, a hull is protected in it's bilge area with fairly small runners (not proper bilge keels). These runners often help to distribute the point loads imposed by bilge rollers on road trailers. The runners are usually tapered top to bottom and at their ends in much the same way as the skeg and can be laminated and fitted in much the same way as the outer stem—Figure 96. It is important to carefully shape and taper the forward and aft ends of the runners so that they create as little

72

turbulence as possible—for a typical runner, say 12' (3.66m) long the tapers should start around 2' (0.61m) from the ends. The ends do not go right down to a point but typically end up 50% of the width and depth of the largest section of the runner.

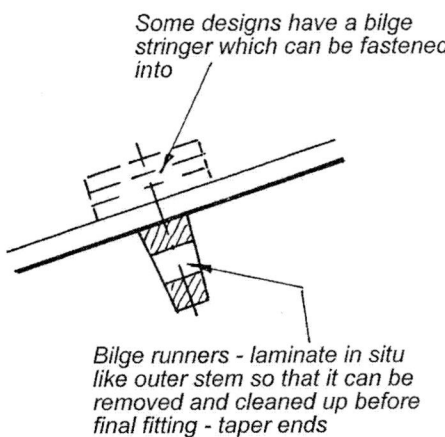

Some designs have a bilge stringer which can be fastened into

Bilge runners - laminate in situ like outer stem so that it can be removed and cleaned up before final fitting - taper ends

Fig 96. Laminated bilge runners.

7.3 Marking the Waterline

Whilst the hull is upside down and level, you may wish to mark the waterline and even paint the bottom of the boat. If the boat is to have a boottop, I wouldn't usually paint this until the hull is upright especially if it is not a parallel line. If you know the height of the waterline from the Reference/Datum line it is quite easy to mark this accurately around the hull. Having marked it, say at the bow, you simply need to get yourself a long clear plastic tube (the type used in fish tanks), fill it with water with a little dye in it and bend this into a 'U' so that you have both ends vertical. The level of the coloured water in both ends of the tube will be exactly the same. If you put one end of the tube up against the mark for the waterline at the bow so that the water level corresponds with that of the waterline mark, wherever you take the other end of the tube along the hull, the level of coloured water in this remote end will also exactly correspond with the waterline mark (Figure 97).

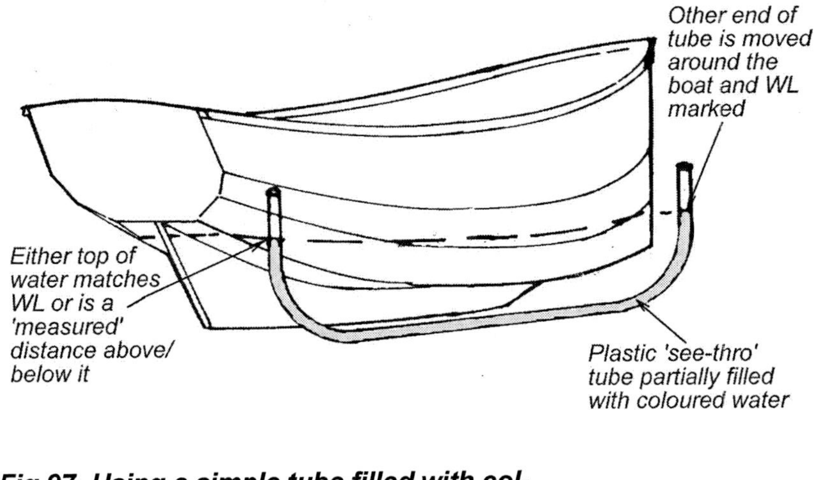

Use this to mark more spots on the hull for the water line which you can then join up to mark the line right round the hull. A modern laser level set up on level platforms is also another easy way to mark the waterline on the hull.

7.4 Turning the Hull Over

Turning the hull over always causes worry but then usually goes very well and is often easier to do than first thought. You will have to look at the space you have for the roll over and if you have not got enough space to one side, you will have to take the hull out of the building shed, turn it over and move it back in again.

The hull suddenly falling over during this process is not a good idea and so I usually have several old mattresses or bails of straw ready to take any impact as the gunwale on one side meets the ground.

Other end of tube is moved around the boat and WL marked

Either top of water matches WL or is a 'measured' distance above/ below it

Plastic 'see-thro' tube partially filled with coloured water

Fig 97. Using a simple tube filled with coloured water to mark the waterline around the hull.

Support the hull on temporary blocks whilst you cut away and remove the strongback and frame supports. If you have the height to have a gantry over the boat from which you can suspend the side that is going to go down onto the floor first, so much the better but otherwise attach 2 or 3 ropes with pulleys to the framework and gunwale on the side to go down and take these ropes over the hull and fasten them to hold fasts in the floor (or part of the building shed) on the opposite side. Even a 30 or 40 foot hull will not weigh too much without the ballast and most of the weight will be taken through the temporary supports to the ground anyway – we just want to control the turn over so that no sudden impact occurs (Figure 98).

With these guide ropes tight and with straw bails or mattresses placed below the gunwale you can carefully knock out the temporary supports on the side to go down. Use the tackles to gently let the gunwale come to the floor. Shift the hull sideways if you can to give yourself some space - take the tackles off the downward gunwale and fix them to the other gunwale and use them to help complete the hull roll over.

Jack up the hull and check that it is level and well supported high enough to allow the filled ballast keel box to be slid underneath before the hull is lowered carefully onto it.

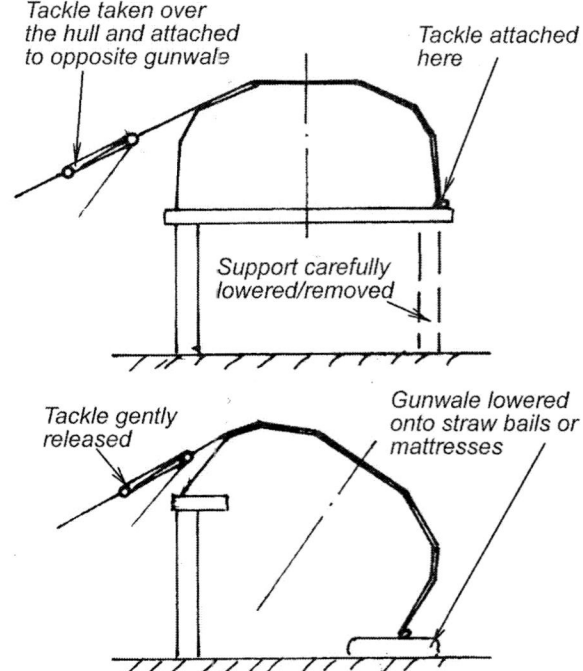

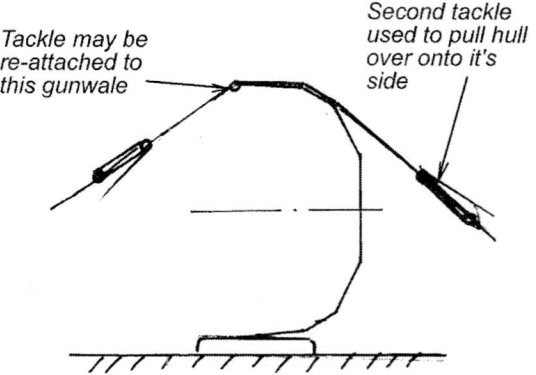

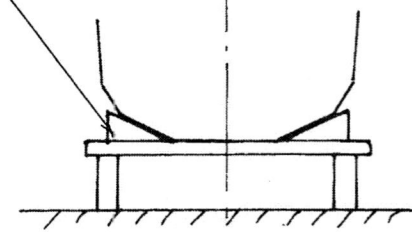

Fig 98. Turning the hull over.

Left—turning the hull of Sam Watt's Selway Fisher CR25 over.

Chapter 8

DECK STRUCTURE
SUPERSTRUCTURE & DECK JOINERY

8.1 Decking

8.1.1 The Deck Structure

We will assume that the tops of the athwartship (side to side) plywood frames/bulkheads and fore and aft plywood girders have been cut over height leaving material to be trimmed. For the main deck there are 2 important items to consider – the position of the carlin which defines the plan shape of the coachhouse coaming and the shape of the beams (Figure 99).

I normally start by establishing the position and shape of all of the full beams and then work forward and aft of these for the remaining deck structure. If the deck is to be flat and have no camber, then life is simple and your main complete beam just forward of the coachhouse can be positioned and simply housed into the inwales (Figure 100).

Most yachts have cambered decks, partly for strength and stiffness and also to help shed water off the deck. Establishing the camber curve and therefore the amount of curve for each beam is not too difficult once the camber curve has been established. Each boatyard would have a different way of drawing the camber curve – some quite complicated. The problem is, that as well as the width of beam changing as you go forward and aft on the hull, the sheer curve (side profile of the gunwale) changes too. Some builders have quite involved ways of dealing with this but, frankly, so long as you are willing to make small individual adjustments to the curve of the beams,

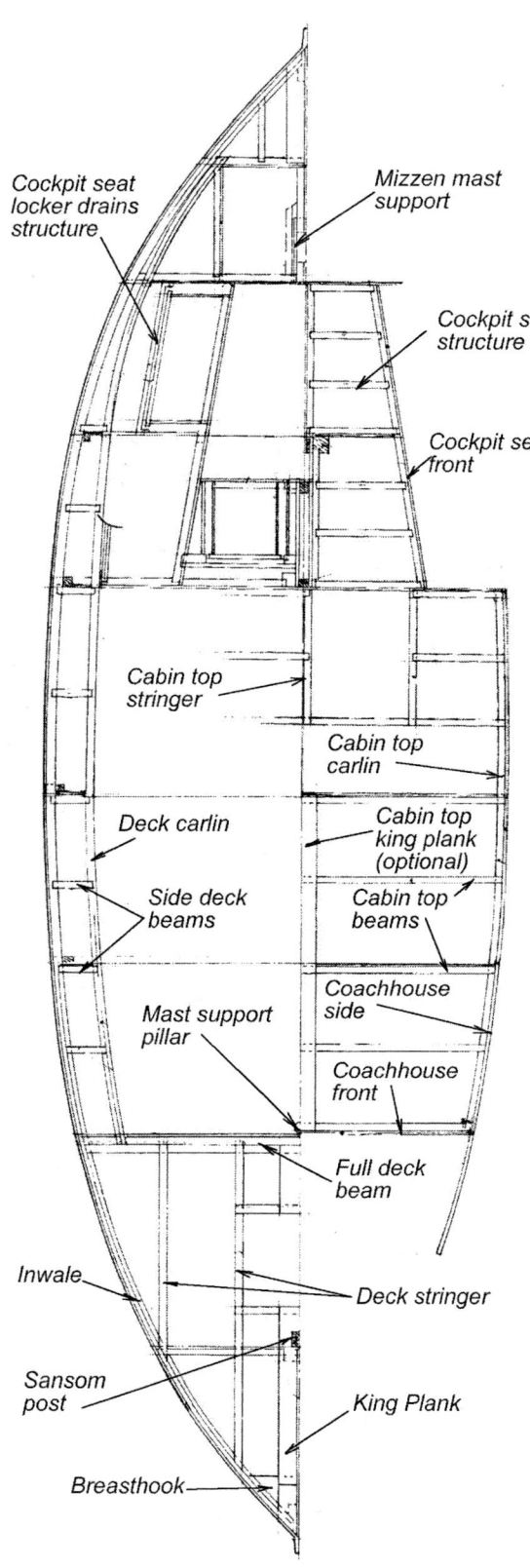

Fig 99. The deck construction plan for the Selway Fisher Kari 4—25'1' (7.65m) double ended cruising yacht.

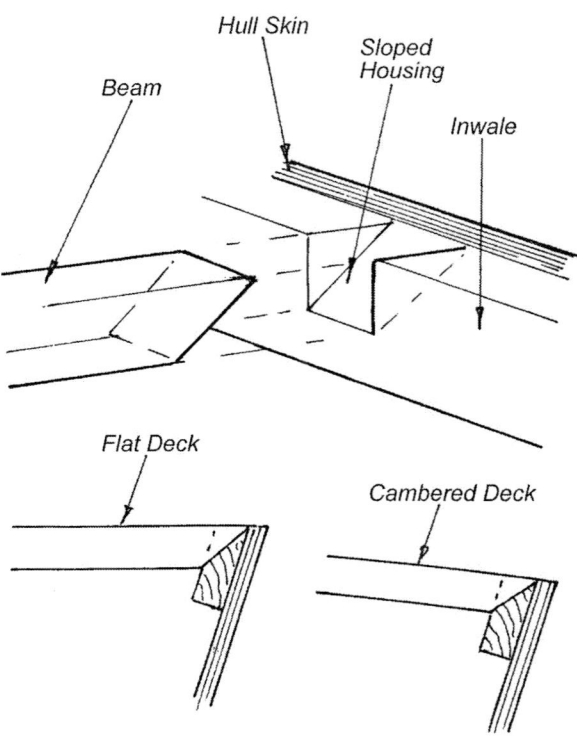

Fig 100. Housing a deck beam into the gunwale for a deck without camber.

judiciously using a plane, I stick with a fairly simple method.

First a plywood or scrap wood template is made of the full camber curve. The camber should be marked on the deck construction drawing. Typically for a 24' (7.32m) long boat it will be something like 2 3/4" (70mm in 8' (2.44m) of beam. This means that the maximum depth of the camber (the height of the camber hill, so to speak) is 2 3/4" at a maximum hull beam of 8' – the actual beam of the boat may be slightly less than 8' but this does not matter. As the camber goes forward and the beam reduces, so the camber height reduces until right at the tip of the bow, where there is no beam, there is also no camber.

To make up the template for the camber curve draw a straight line on your template material and at it's centre point raise a perpendicular line. Where these two lines meet use this as the centre of a semi-circle with a radius equal to the maximum camber height. For the length of the horizontal line left and right of this centre mark off your 4' (1/2 beam) and divide these distances into 4 equal parts and raise perpendicular lines (1,2 and 3) at these points.

From the centre of the semi-circle draw lines at 45, 22 ½ and 67 ½ degrees to cut the circle at points a,b and c. Divide the horizontal radius of the circle into 4 equal parts marked x,y and z. the length of the lines x-a, y-b and z-c are then transferred to the lines 1.2 and 3 and the points joined up in a curve – do the same on the other side and you now have your complete camber curve. Finally, carefully cut this curve out preserving the top part which is now your camber template.

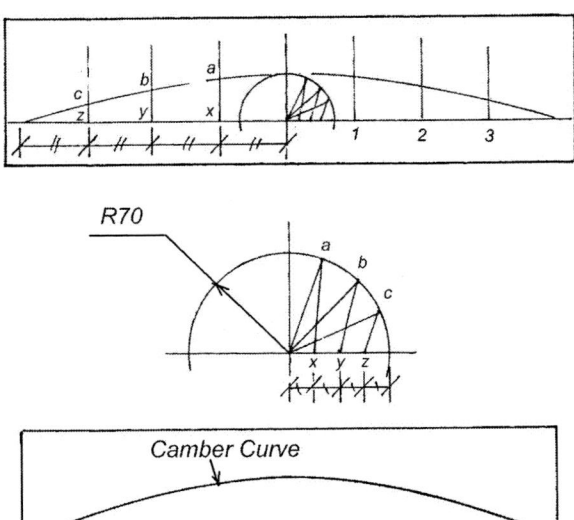

Fig 101. Drawing the camber curve and making a template.

All you now do is rest this template across the gunwales at any point along the length of the hull and you have the curve and camber

height at that point – it will give you the shape of any beam at whatever point you position the curve along the length of the boat (Figure 102). The strongest and least wasteful

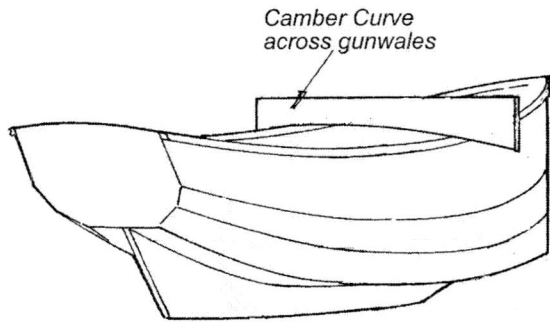

Fig 102. Using the camber curve along the length of the boat.

way to make up a cambered deck beam is to laminate it – once the camber curve has been established for a particular beam, it can laminated in a number of ways. Here is just one method, where the curve is drawn down onto thick chipboard base and the curve is defined by a series of steel angle brackets bolted to the base so that their faces lie perpendicularly from the curve. Laminates can then be clamped to these steel with glue between them whilst the glue cures (Figure 103).

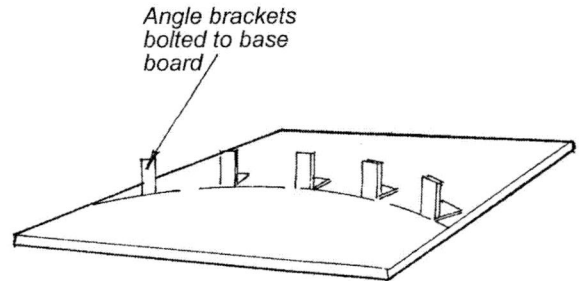

Fig 103. Laminating the deck beams.

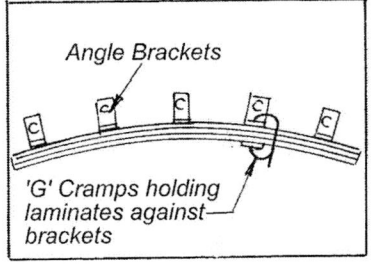

If the brackets are a foot (0.3m) or so tall, several beams can be laminated at the same time as the curve remains the same for most of the beams – it is just the width that changes. Once the beams have been laminated, they can be removed from the jig and cleaned up ready to have their ends shaped to fit the join into the inwale (Figure 104).

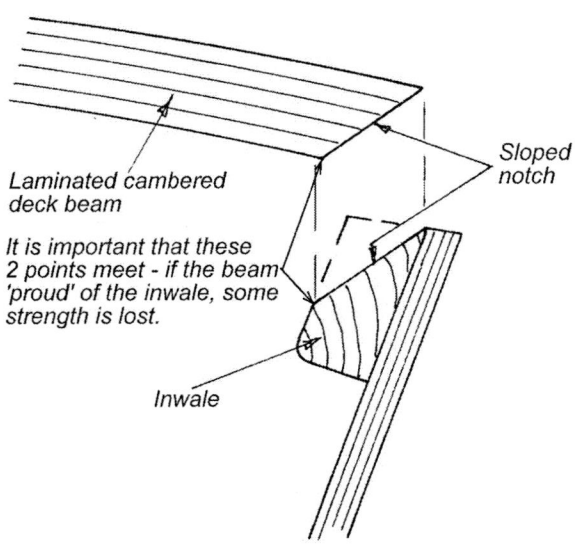

Fig 104. Housing the beams into the gunwale for cambered beams.

For both cambered and un-cambered decks, it is very important that the bottom of the cut and shaped end of the beams does not lie 'proud' of the inwale—this will mean that the beam is unable to use all it's stiffness and strength to support the deck. Sometimes the end of the beam is housed further into the inwale with a horizontal 'landing' cut onto the bottom of the notch cut into the inwale. However, this will weaken the inwale more than necessary, remember, it is always necessary to design the join so that we retain the structural integrity and stiffness of both items being joined.

As a compromise and in view of the need not to ruin the structural integrity of the inwale by cutting too much out of it, some builders use a 'double' sloped join—see the deck edge detail in Figure 119.

An alternative way to make cambered beams is simply to cut them from the solid plank but if they are shaped on their underside, this gives them short grain areas which are weak (Figure 105).

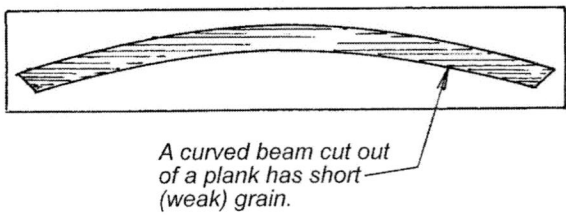

Fig 105. A weak cambered beam cut from a solid plank.

If the beam is up against a bulkhead then there is no reason why the bottom cannot be kept flat which avoids this problem and makes for an easily shaped beam (Figure 106).

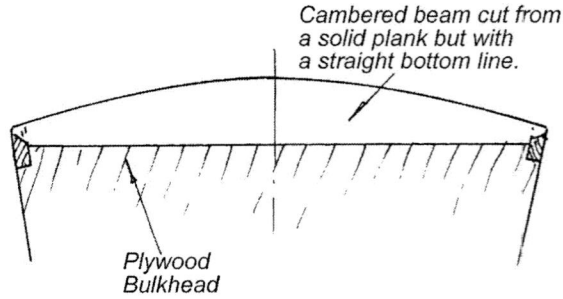

Fig 106. An easy way to fit a beam against a plywood frame/bulkhead—cut from solid plank with a flat bottom so that there is no short grain.

There will almost certainly not be a continuous beam across the aft end of the coachhouse because of the cockpit and companion entrance – but the beam camber template can be used here to gain the shape of the plywood bulkhead above the gunwale – the same can be done at any other intermediate bulkheads (Figure 107) – and these partial beams can be made up and fixed to the bulkheads.

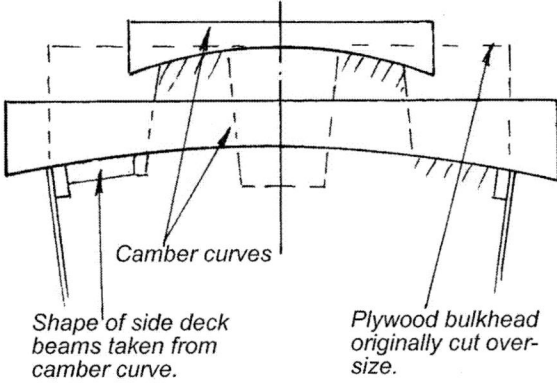

Camber curves

Shape of side deck beams taken from camber curve.

Plywood bulkhead originally cut over-size.

Fig 107. Marking the deck and cabin shape of the companion bulkhead.

If there are intermediate bulkheads running up under the side decks this makes it easier for establishing how the carlin runs and also for fixing it in place. If there are no intermediate bulkheads, the carlin needs to be fixed in position using simple plywood clamps – the width of the side deck at various points should be given on the drawings (Figure 108).

The carlins can then be laminated either permanently in place or, so that they can be more easily cleaned up on the bench, dry fitted to the beams.

King planks and under deck blocking such as the breast hook can now be fitted and any specific blocks used for particular deck fittings can also be fitted in place. The whole deck structure should then be faired and cleaned up. You may want to do any final sanding and even varnishing/painting of the deck structure now, before the deck itself goes on – it is much easier at this stage, but do keep paints etc off the top surface of the deck structure where it will be glued to the decking.

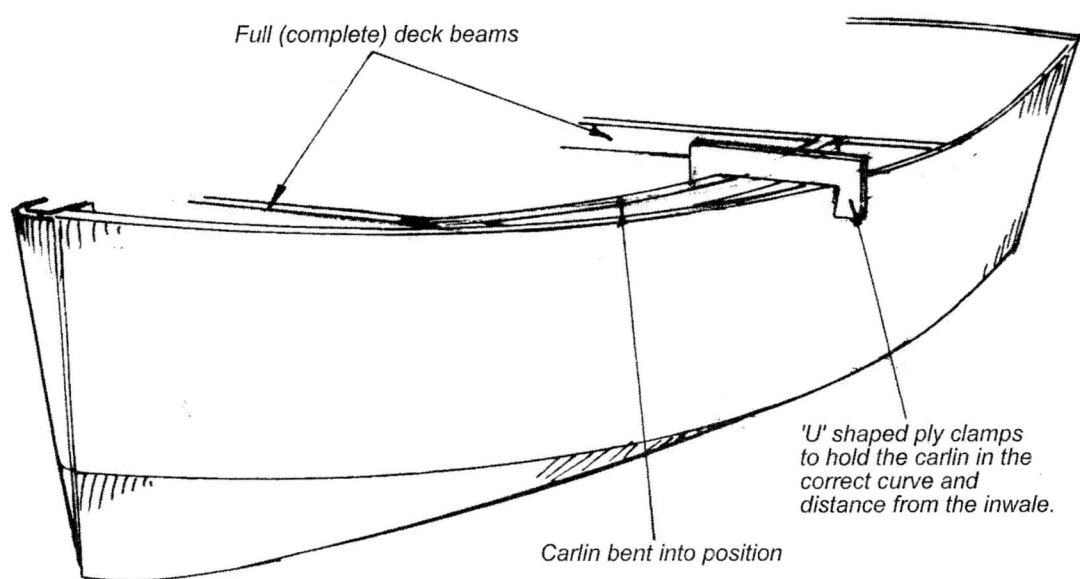

Full (complete) deck beams

'U' shaped ply clamps to hold the carlin in the correct curve and distance from the inwale.

Carlin bent into position

Fig 108. Holding the deck carlin in place.

8.1.2 The Cockpit

If you have not already done so, the cockpit should be fitted now. If there is an inboard engine, fit this first, but then make sure that it is well covered and protected and that all open ports in the engine are well blocked off to keep sawdust and debris out! Diesel tanks, fresh water tanks and possibly some plumbing may also be fitted at this stage. In fact some builders do much of the interior fit-out before the decking and coachhouse goes on – this is often a sensible way to work, but make sure that everything you do on the interior at this stage, is well protected.

You should always plan the cockpit so that major machinery can be removed through it, later, for maintenance – *do not build items in permanently, if you can avoid it!* An easy solution, assuming that the inboard engine is below the cockpit, is to make the whole cockpit sole removable by bedding it onto it's supporting structure and holding it down with bolts or screws in cup washers. Cockpit sole beams can be made removable in much the same way (Figure 109).

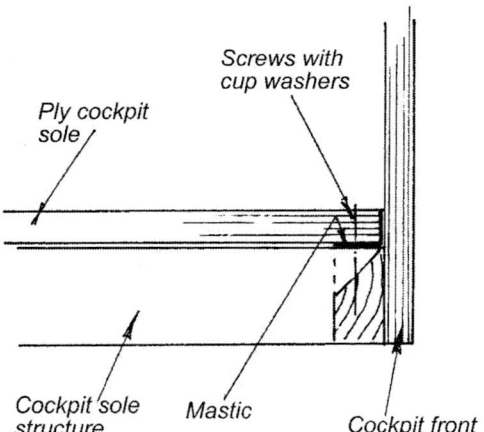

Fig 109. Removable cockpit sole.

Fuel tanks are often tucked up out of the way under the side decks but if you can position these so that they can be removed too, so much the better.

8.1.3 The Deck

There is a question as to whether the deck or the coachhouse sides should be fitted next. There are certainly advantages to fitting the coachhouse sides from the point of view of easily fastening it to the carlin, but I prefer to fit the deck first just so that I do not damage the coachhouse sides when finishing the deck.

We will assume that the deck itself is plywood with perhaps, a layer of Teak decking on top. Solid laid Teak or Pitch Pine decks are fine and there are many older books that cover their construction but, as this is a book concerning larger plywood boats, it would seem ridiculous to ignore the fact that there are several advantages in at least having a plywood 'under deck'. A plywood deck acts as a massive strength member by imparting to the plan-form shape of the boat, stiffness and stability in shape. Rather than having individual planks running fore and aft, we have a sheet stiffener and strength member tying all parts of the deck together in the horizontal plane. Having spent many a sleepless night under a leaking laid deck, a plywood deck makes life dry!

The ply deck may go on in one thickness or in several thicknesses if there is a lot of camber – the rules and comments we used for the hull planking apply here. If the plywood is applied in several layers then joins in successive layers should be staggered – if not and only one thickness is applied, I like to use butt straps much like those for the hull planking. Of course, if there is blocking under the deck, these can act as butt straps too.

Some builders arrange joins in the plywood over the beams and stagger the joins – this is good practice so long as there is a large enough glue area to prevent movement (Figure 110).

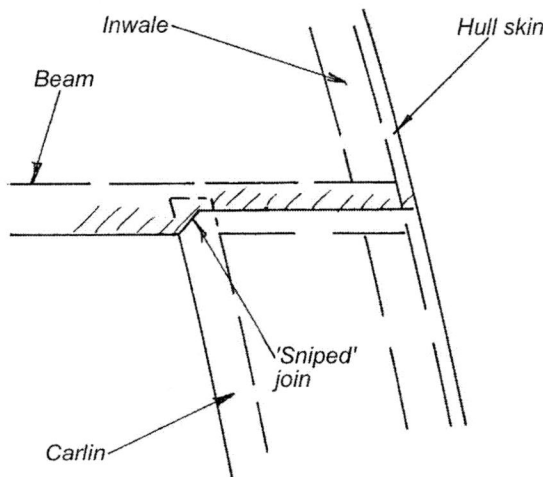

Fig 110. Plywood deck joins.

A typical layout for the plywood deck panels on a single thickness ply deck is shown in Figure 111.

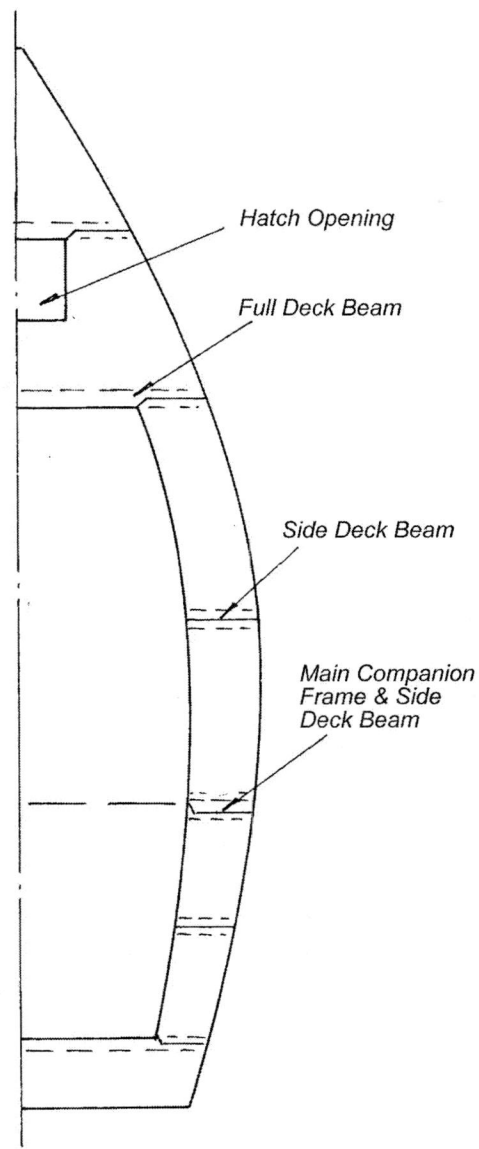

Fig 111. Layout of joins in deck plywood.

8.1.3.1 Sheathed Deck Covering

A simple plywood deck may be finished with a layer of course woven roving in epoxy resin. The same rules used for glass sheathing the hull, apply here except that you want to use a course weave cloth (300 gm or more) and leave the weave unfilled to give the deck some grip.

Do this sheathing before toerails etc are fitted and fit these items over the top of the sheathing (Figure 112).

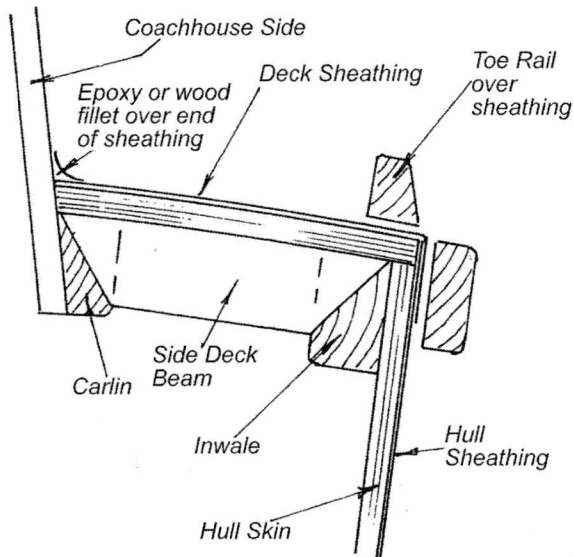

Fig 112. Sheathing the deck.

8.1.3.2 Teak Deck Covering

If you want a deck to be truly proud of, which shows off your craftsmanship, a plywood deck with Teak laid over it, is a good way to go. It is up to you how you want the Teak 'planks' to lie (Figure 113).

There is no need for the strips to be any thicker than 1/8" (3mm) or 3/16" (4mm) and 2" (50mm) wide is fine for most decks. Thicker teak is not necessarily a good idea as in contracting and expanding at a slightly different rate to the plywood under deck, the thicker strips may 'over-power' the epoxy glues used to stick them down.

Before the days of epoxy, the Yard I used to work for, would glue the Teak strips down using a Resorcinal glue and then fill the gaps between the Teak planks with a black butyl rubber compound. It was thought essential to

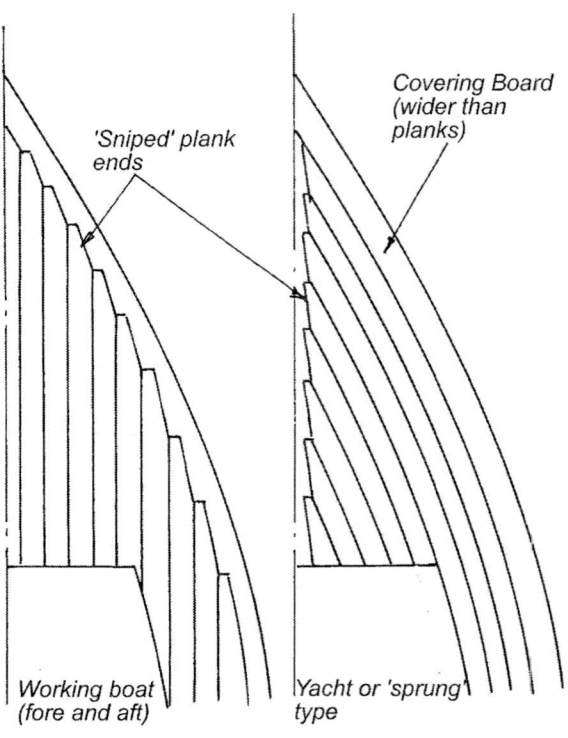

Fig 113. Two of the main ways of laying a

make sure that the butyl rubber did not stick to the plywood surface at the bottom of the gap as this would cause problems with the differentials expansion between the Teak and plywood. To prevent adhesion to the bottom of the gap, cassette tape was laid down in the gap first.

With epoxies, the ideal way to lay the Teak is to glue it down with a thickened mix of epoxy with graphite added to it (often around 10% by volume) – this colours the mix black and the epoxy is allowed to squeeze between the planks and take on the roll of the black filler.

The procedure is to lay the planks out dry, cutting them to shape if possible. With planks that follow the mouth line (plan view curve of the gunwale), this is not always possible

82

and so you simply have to glue and fasten individual planks and make up small quantities of the epoxy/graphite mix as you go. The planks are best fixed in place with ½" (12mm) long staples – use as few staples as possible and staple over old flex so that they can be more easily withdrawn after the epoxy has cured. Use small strips of 5mm thick aluminium to help maintain a 5mm gap between the planks.

Make sure the seams are all filled, allow the epoxy to cure fully and sand with a belt sander using 50 grit paper, finishing with 80 grit paper.

8.2 Coachhouses, Cabin Tops and Superstructures

You may find it helpful to 'mock' the coachhouse coaming and top up in hardboard so that you can check the shape and position of the ports (windows). In any case, a template will need to be taken of the coachhouse coaming (side) from the boat. Traditionally, the side of the coachhouse was often fitted outside a separate coaming to help make a water-tight join but now, with efficient glues, these 2 items are more often combined (Figure 114).

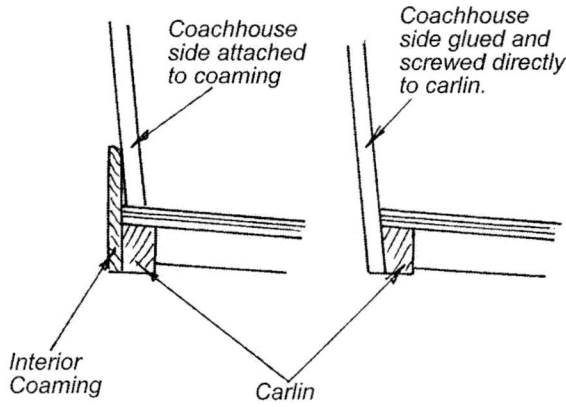

Fig 114. Traditional and modern methods of attaching the coachhouse sides.

There are several ways in which the coachhouse sides and top can be finished off and these are down on Figure 115.

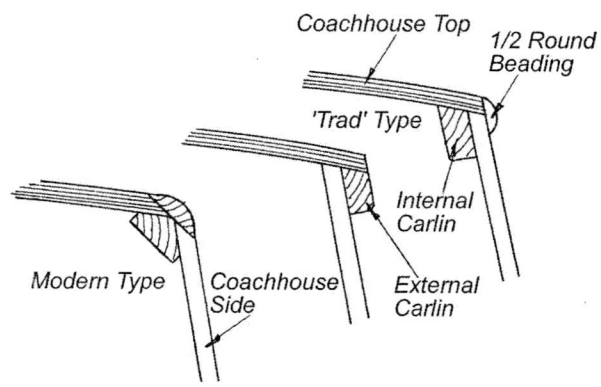

Fig 115. Different ways of joining the coachhouse sides and top.

Coachhouse sides may be plywood or solid wood (Mahogany was often used in the best yacht work) although using solid wood is very expensive in that you need to use wide and very high quality boards. Alternatively, you can strip plank the sides or, as in many American Catboats and Tugboats, use vertical wood staves which may be tongue and groove (Figure 116). Fairly thin tongue and groove staves can be used over and glued to a thin ply inner layer of plywood. The rounded fronts of Catboat cabins were often vertically staved.

Finishing and connecting the front to the sides of the coachhouse also have several different alternatives (Figure 117).

Cabin tops are often highly cambered and therefore have to be applied in 2 or 3 layers of thin plywood. If the top is of a highly 'compound' shape (with curves fore and aft and athwartship), the layers of plywood may need to be put on in diagonal strips around 5" (125mm) wide. The whole top can be finished off with a glass sheathing. If the top

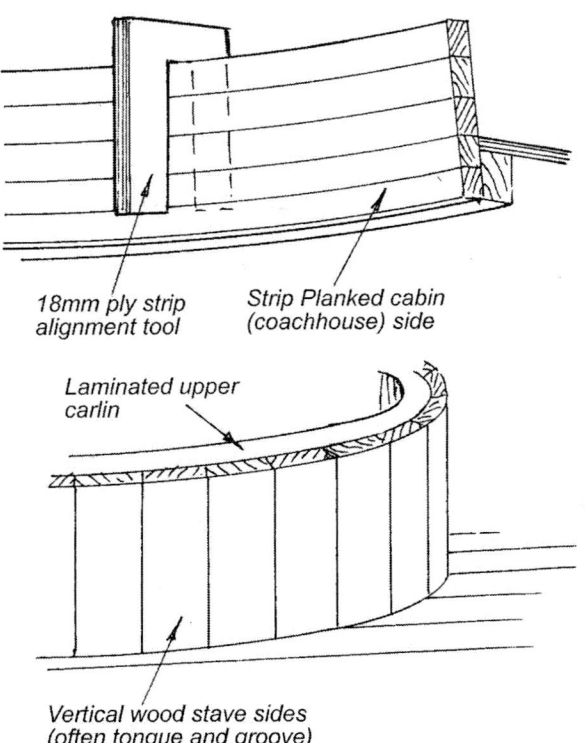

18mm ply strip
alignment tool

Strip Planked cabin
(coachhouse) side

Laminated upper
carlin

Vertical wood stave sides
(often tongue and groove)

Fig 116. Strip planked and vertically staved coachhouse sides.

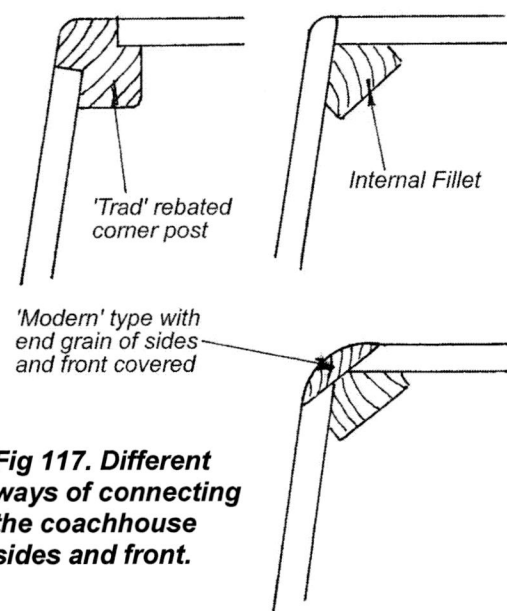

'Trad' rebated
corner post

Internal Fillet

'Modern' type with
end grain of sides
and front covered

Fig 117. Different ways of connecting the coachhouse sides and front.

The pictures on this and page 87 are of the cabin on Graham Young's Selway Fisher Tideway 14 under construction.

is applied using this diagonal method, it is quite likely that fore and aft stringers will need to be fitted first, in order to give enough support to the thin diagonal plywood planking (Figure 118). The actual plywood top is, when fully glued, very stiff and strong—therefore, if you need to save weight or require a few inches more headroom it is often possible to remove many of the supporting beam and stringers after the top is finished. The easiest way to do this, is to consider the beams etc as temporary during construction and fit them to the coachhouse carlin temporarily. The top would be laminated in situ but not glued to the supporting structure. The top is then removed, those beams and stringers that can be taken out, removed and the top glued and fastened back in place.

Coachhouse tops may also be strip planked. Fore and aft stringers are not required but maybe, more temporary beams/moulds are. The strip planked top may be treated in the same way as the diagonally planked top and be removed, so that some beams can be taken out of the structure and also so that the underside of the top may be sheathed in glass. This makes a very stiff and strong shell top (Figure 118).

If the coachhouse top is applied in one thickness, the layout of the joins is much the same as used for the main deck with joins made over beams. If it is put on in two or more thicknesses, stagger the joins.

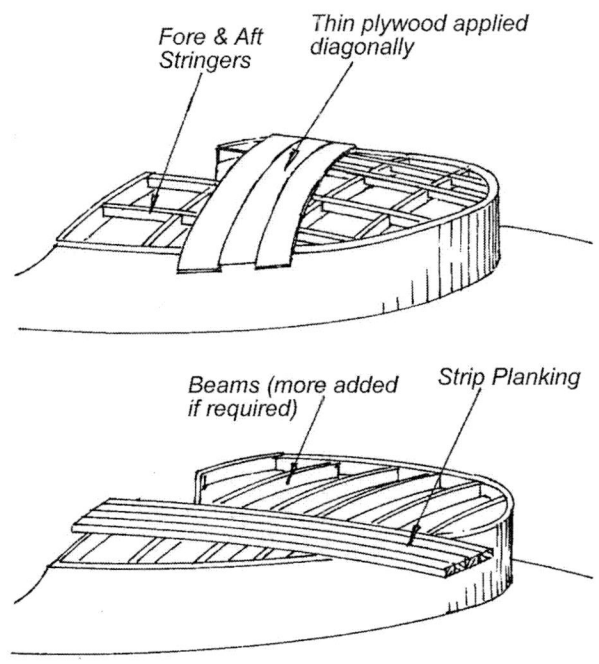

Fore & Aft Stringers

Thin plywood applied diagonally

Beams (more added if required)

Strip Planking

Fig 118—above. Diagonally planked and strip planked coachhouse tops.

8.3 Companion Hatches & Typical Deck Joinery

Figures 119 to 131 give sample details of typical joinery to fit-out decks. There are many more resources detailing the construction of these items, but those given here are fairly simple examples of how to construct wood deck ware, for yourself.

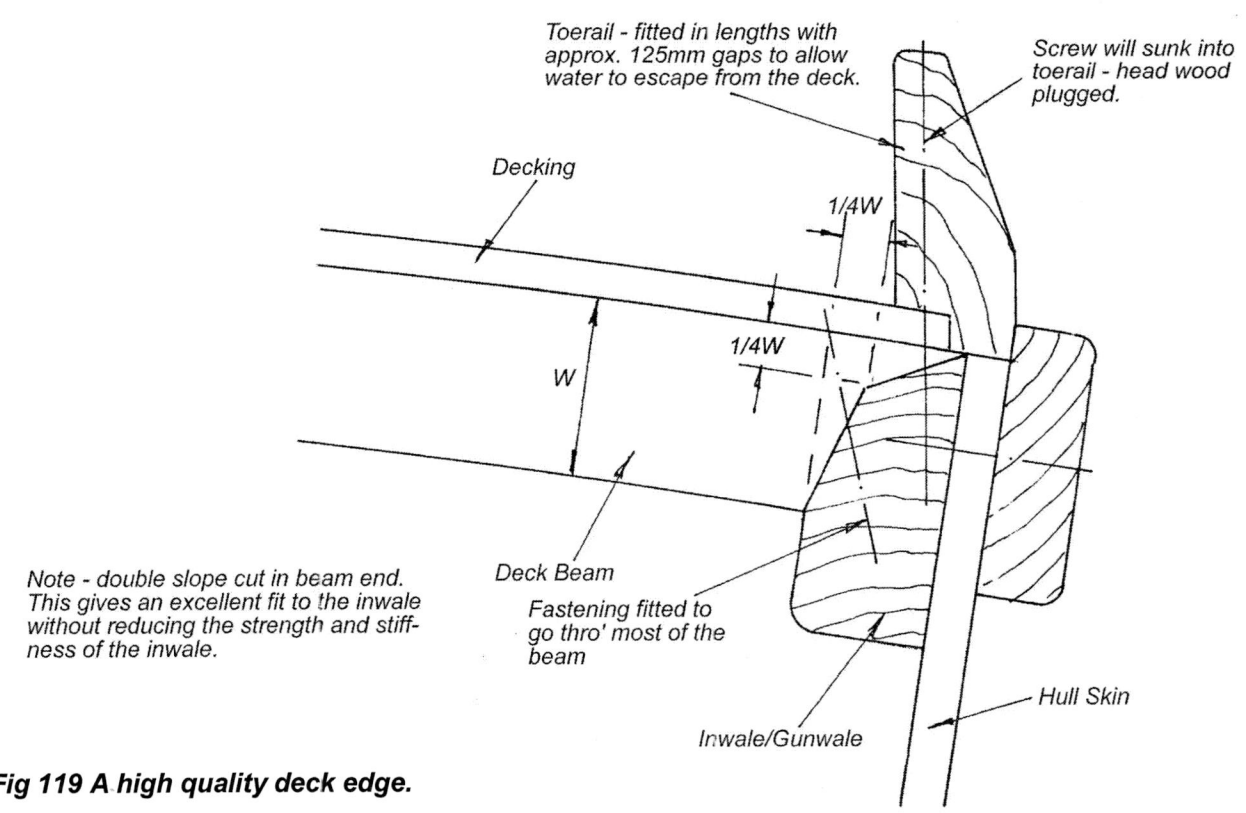

Toerail - fitted in lengths with approx. 125mm gaps to allow water to escape from the deck.

Screw will sunk into toerail - head wood plugged.

Decking

1/4W

1/4W

W

Note - double slope cut in beam end. This gives an excellent fit to the inwale without reducing the strength and stiffness of the inwale.

Deck Beam

Fastening fitted to go thro' most of the beam

Inwale/Gunwale

Hull Skin

Fig 119 A high quality deck edge.

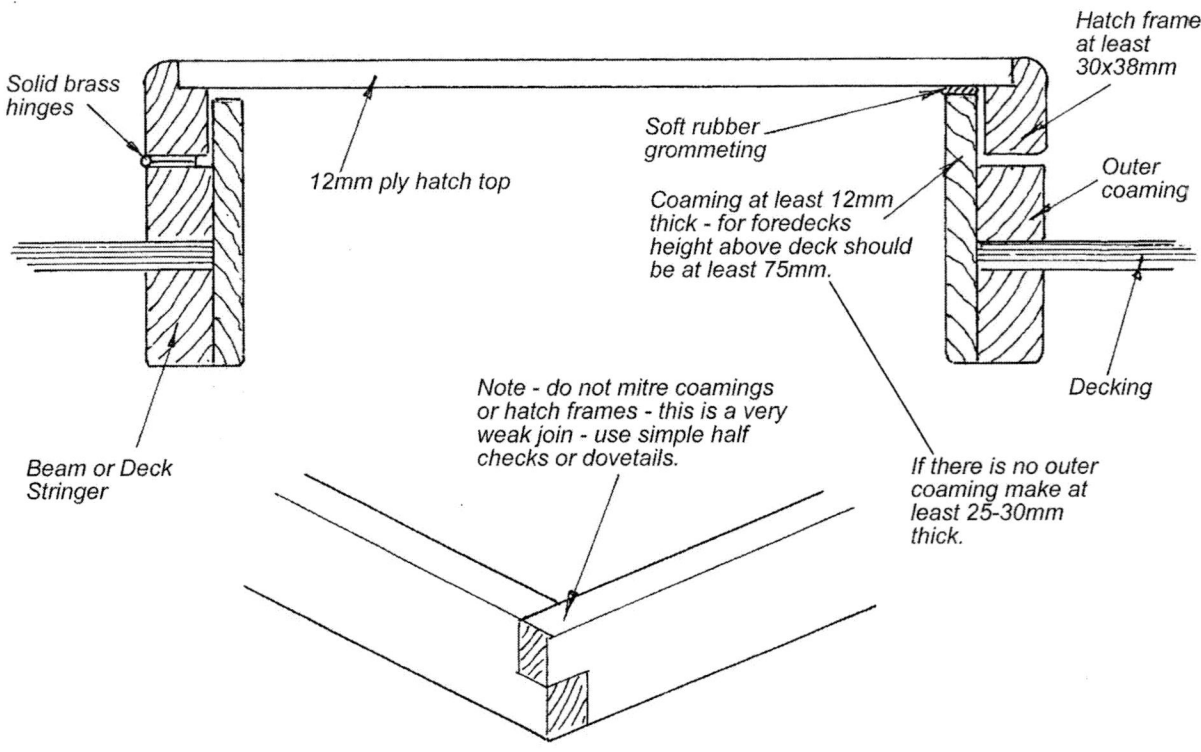

Fig 120. Deck hatch construction.

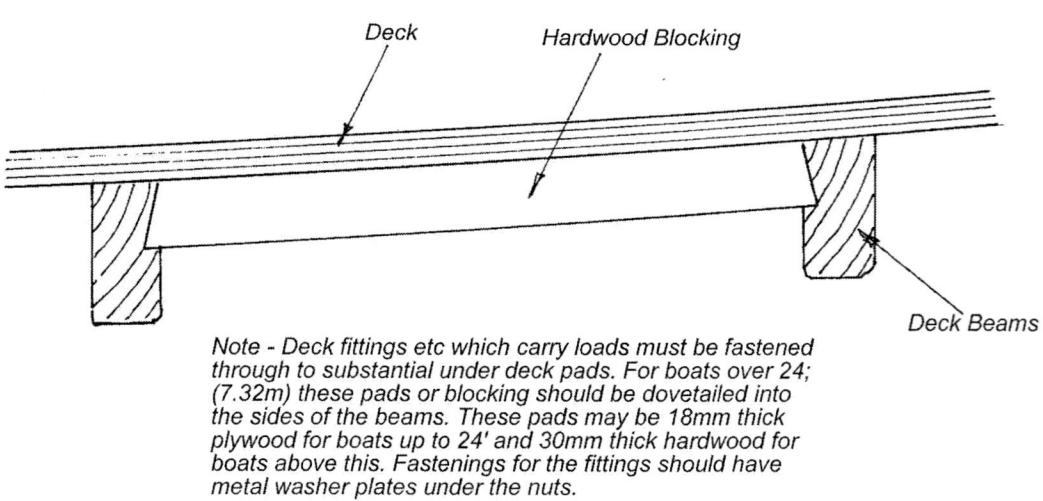

Note - Deck fittings etc which carry loads must be fastened through to substantial under deck pads. For boats over 24; (7.32m) these pads or blocking should be dovetailed into the sides of the beams. These pads may be 18mm thick plywood for boats up to 24' and 30mm thick hardwood for boats above this. Fastenings for the fittings should have metal washer plates under the nuts.

Fig 121. Deck blocking for fittings fastened to the deck.

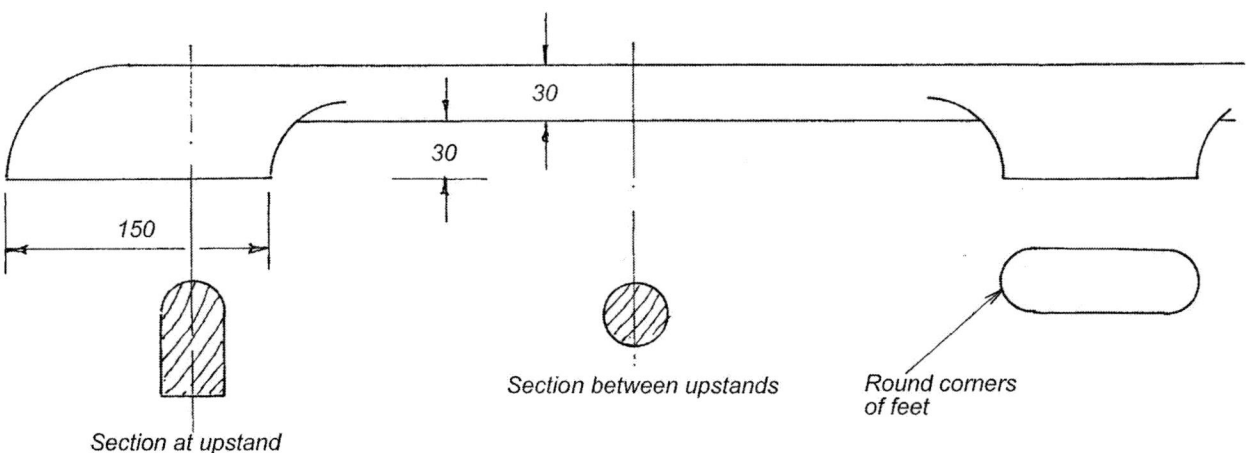

150

30

30

Section at upstand

Section between upstands

Round corners of feet

Fig 122. Coachhouse top handrails (Teak).

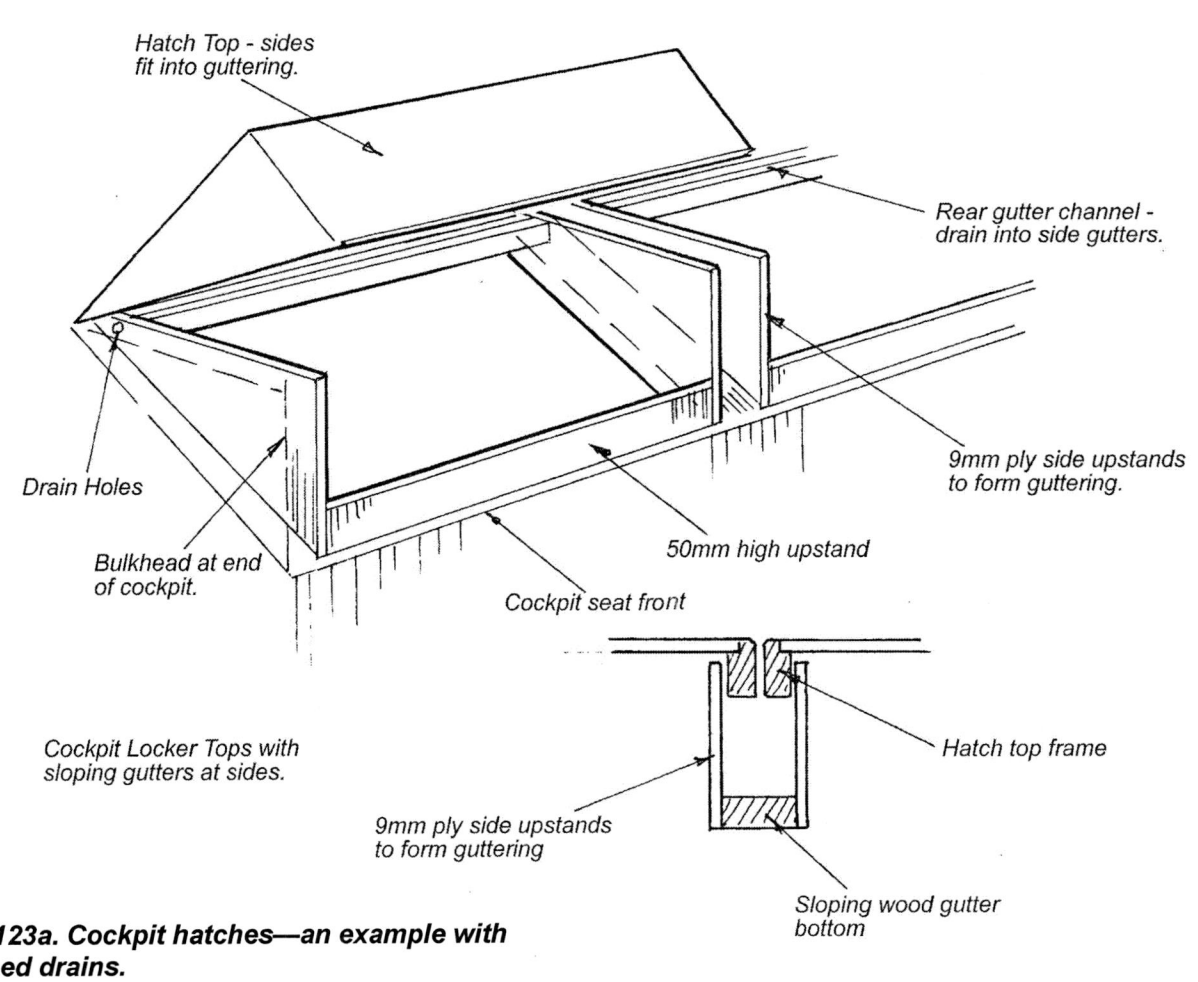

Hatch Top - sides fit into guttering.

Rear gutter channel - drain into side gutters.

Drain Holes

Bulkhead at end of cockpit.

Cockpit seat front

50mm high upstand

9mm ply side upstands to form guttering.

Cockpit Locker Tops with sloping gutters at sides.

9mm ply side upstands to form guttering

Hatch top frame

Sloping wood gutter bottom

Fig 123a. Cockpit hatches—an example with sloped drains.

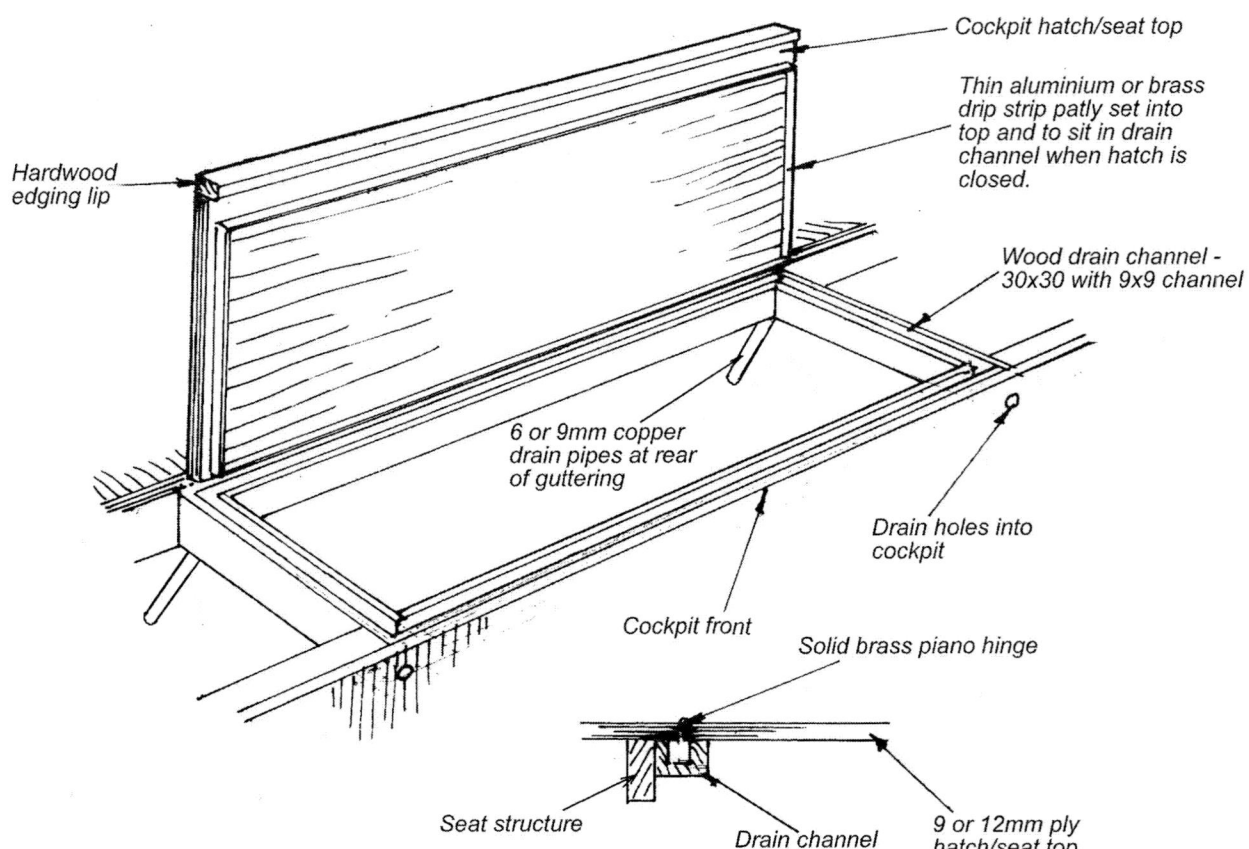

Cockpit hatch/seat top

Thin aluminium or brass drip strip patly set into top and to sit in drain channel when hatch is closed.

Hardwood edging lip

Wood drain channel - 30x30 with 9x9 channel

6 or 9mm copper drain pipes at rear of guttering

Drain holes into cockpit

Cockpit front

Solid brass piano hinge

Seat structure

Drain channel

9 or 12mm ply hatch/seat top

Fig 123b. Cockpit hatches—an example with flat gutters.

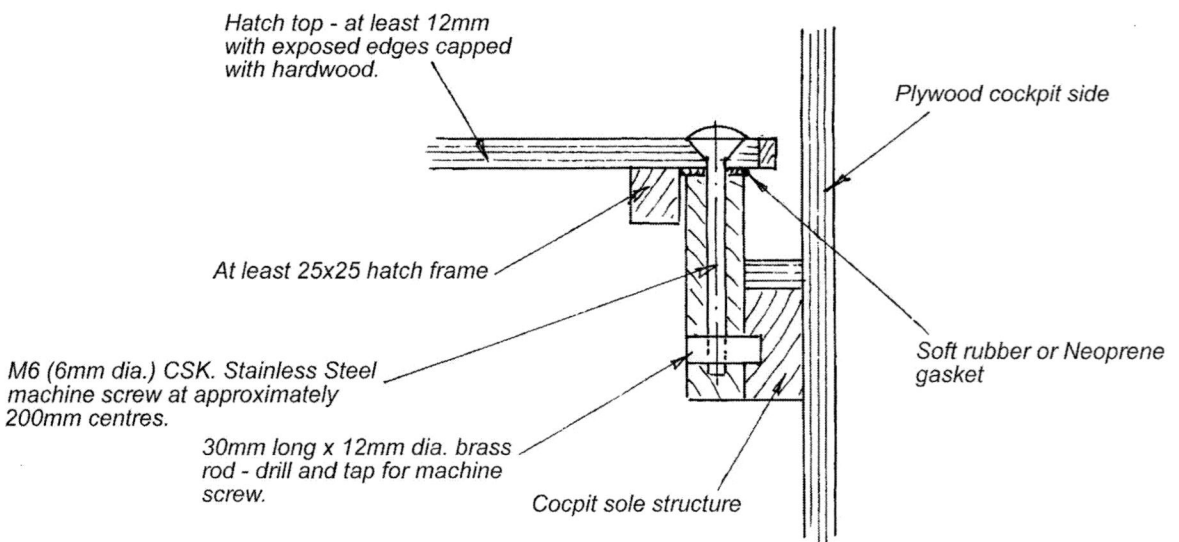

Hatch top - at least 12mm with exposed edges capped with hardwood.

Plywood cockpit side

At least 25x25 hatch frame

M6 (6mm dia.) CSK. Stainless Steel machine screw at approximately 200mm centres.

Soft rubber or Neoprene gasket

30mm long x 12mm dia. brass rod - drill and tap for machine screw.

Cocpit sole structure

Fig 124. Removable hatch in the cockpit sole for occasional access.

Deck Structure

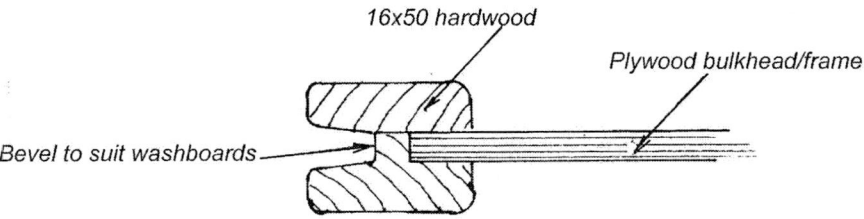

16x50 hardwood

Plywood bulkhead/frame

Bevel to suit washboards

TOP VIEW - VERTICAL SECTION
AT EDGE OF OPENING

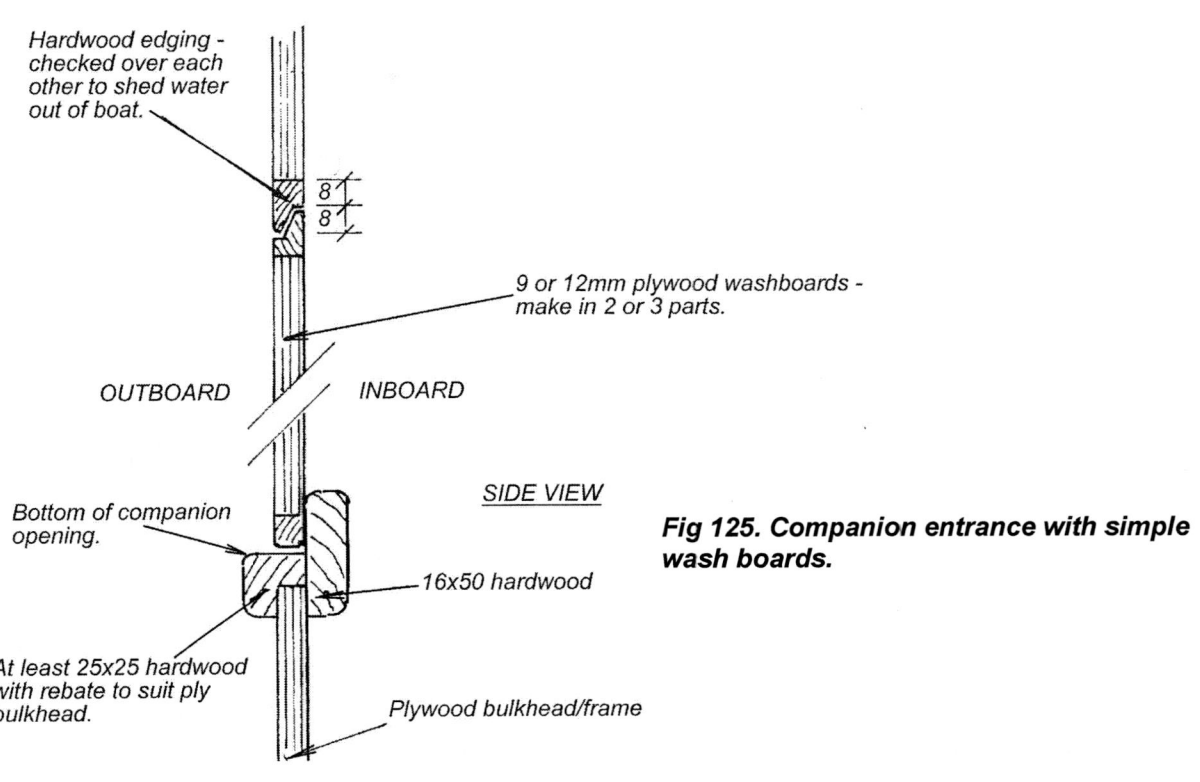

Hardwood edging -
checked over each
other to shed water
out of boat.

8
8

9 or 12mm plywood washboards -
make in 2 or 3 parts.

OUTBOARD   INBOARD

SIDE VIEW

Bottom of companion
opening.

16x50 hardwood

At least 25x25 hardwood
with rebate to suit ply
bulkhead.

Plywood bulkhead/frame

**Fig 125. Companion entrance with simple
wash boards.**

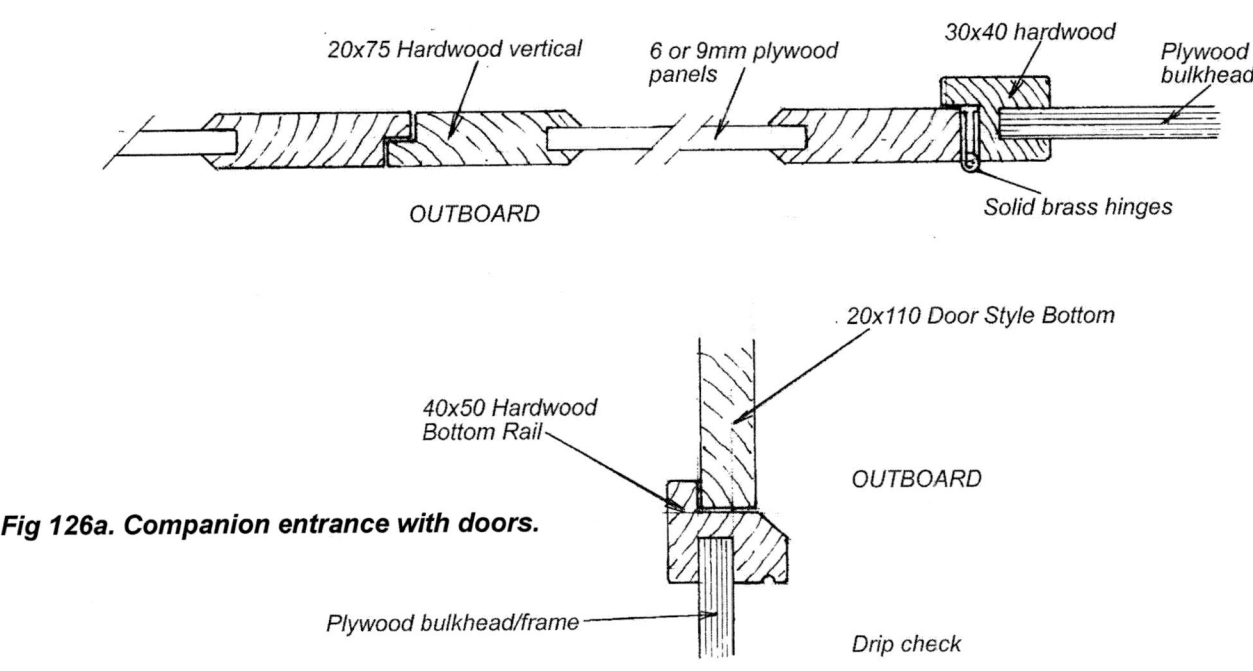

20x75 Hardwood vertical   6 or 9mm plywood
panels

30x40 hardwood

Plywood
bulkhead

OUTBOARD

Solid brass hinges

20x110 Door Style Bottom

40x50 Hardwood
Bottom Rail

OUTBOARD

Fig 126a. Companion entrance with doors.

Plywood bulkhead/frame

Drip check

89

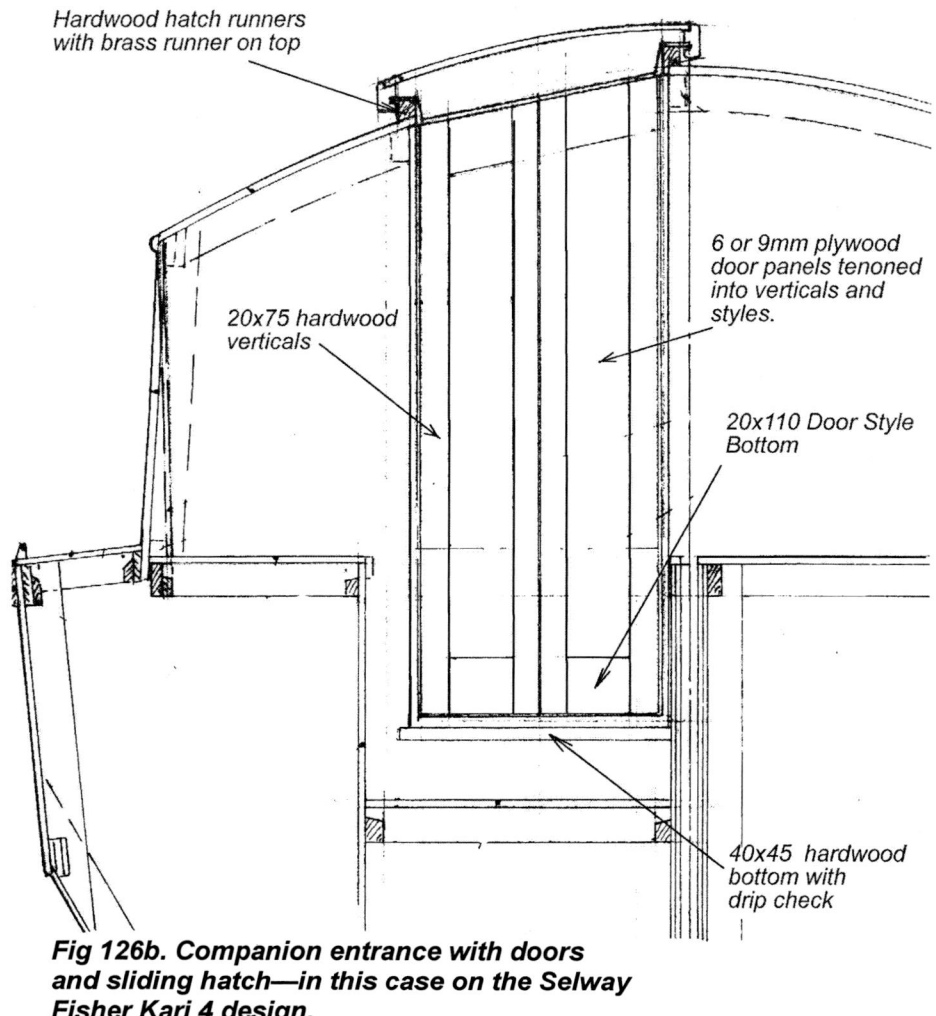

Hardwood hatch runners
with brass runner on top

20x75 hardwood
verticals

6 or 9mm plywood
door panels tenoned
into verticals and
styles.

20x110 Door Style
Bottom

40x45 hardwood
bottom with
drip check

**Fig 126b. Companion entrance with doors
and sliding hatch—in this case on the Selway
Fisher Kari 4 design.**

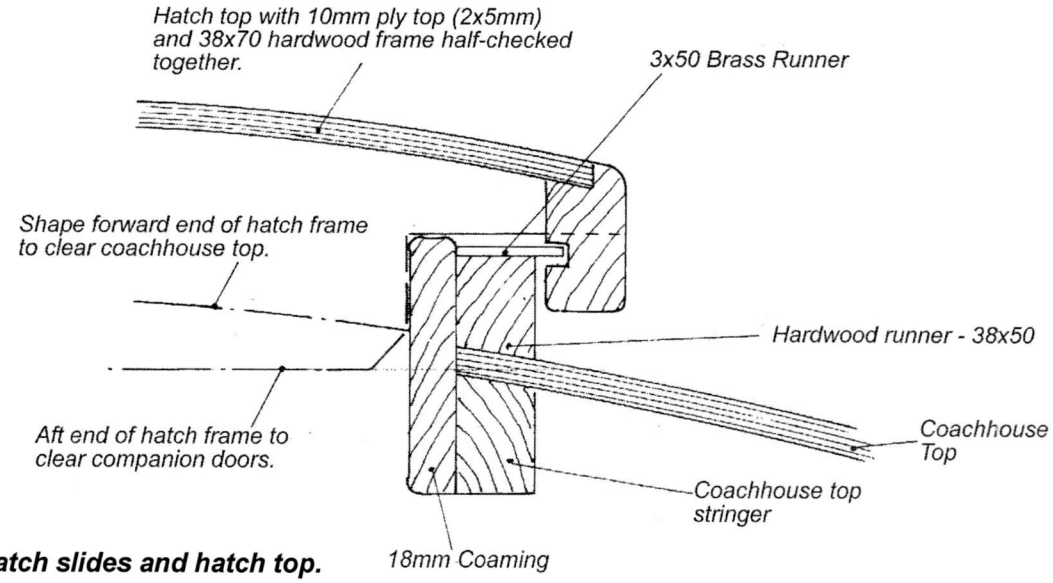

Hatch top with 10mm ply top (2x5mm)
and 38x70 hardwood frame half-checked
together.

3x50 Brass Runner

Shape forward end of hatch frame
to clear coachhouse top.

Hardwood runner - 38x50

Aft end of hatch frame to
clear companion doors.

Coachhouse
Top

Coachhouse top
stringer

18mm Coaming

Fig 127. Typical hatch slides and hatch top.

Deck Structure

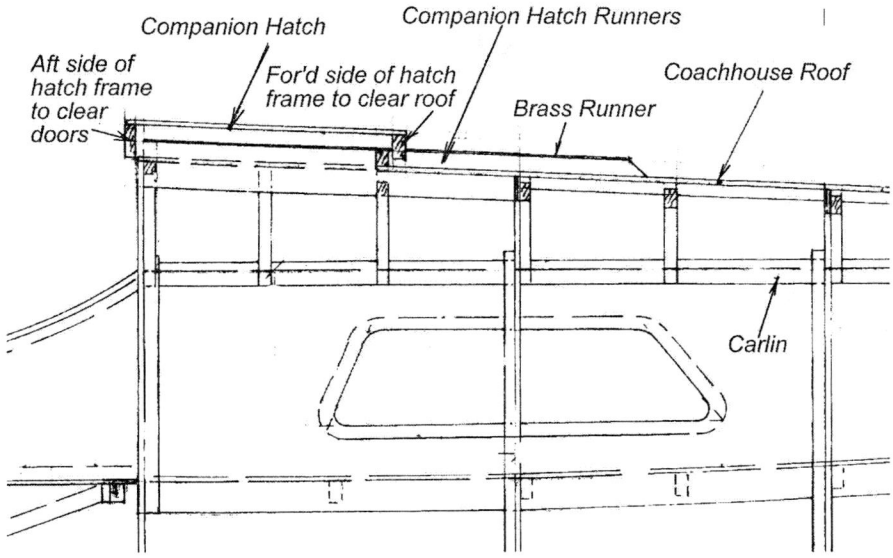

Fig 128. Side view of companion hatch, again for the Kari 4 design.

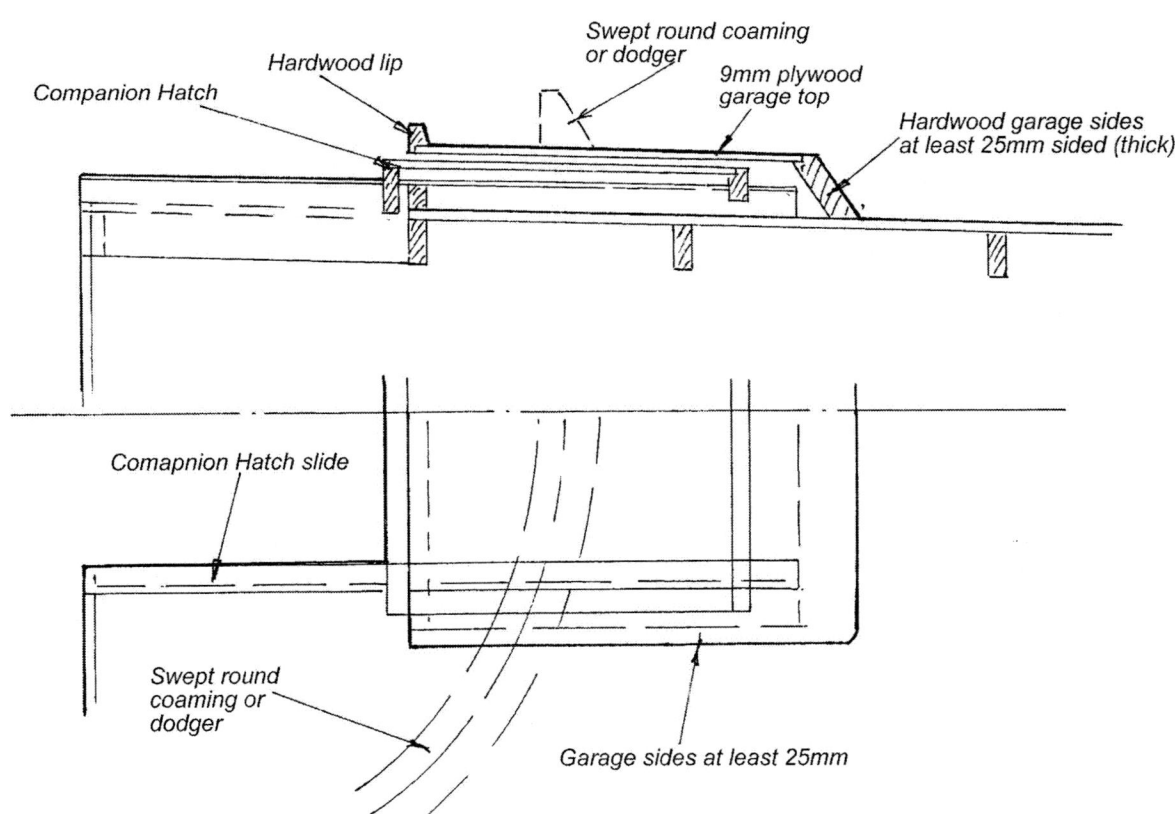

Fig 129. Simple garage for the companion hatch—required if a dodger or wheelhouse is to be built over the hatch or, the cockpit coaming is swept up and over the cabin top to form a water break.

Deck Structure

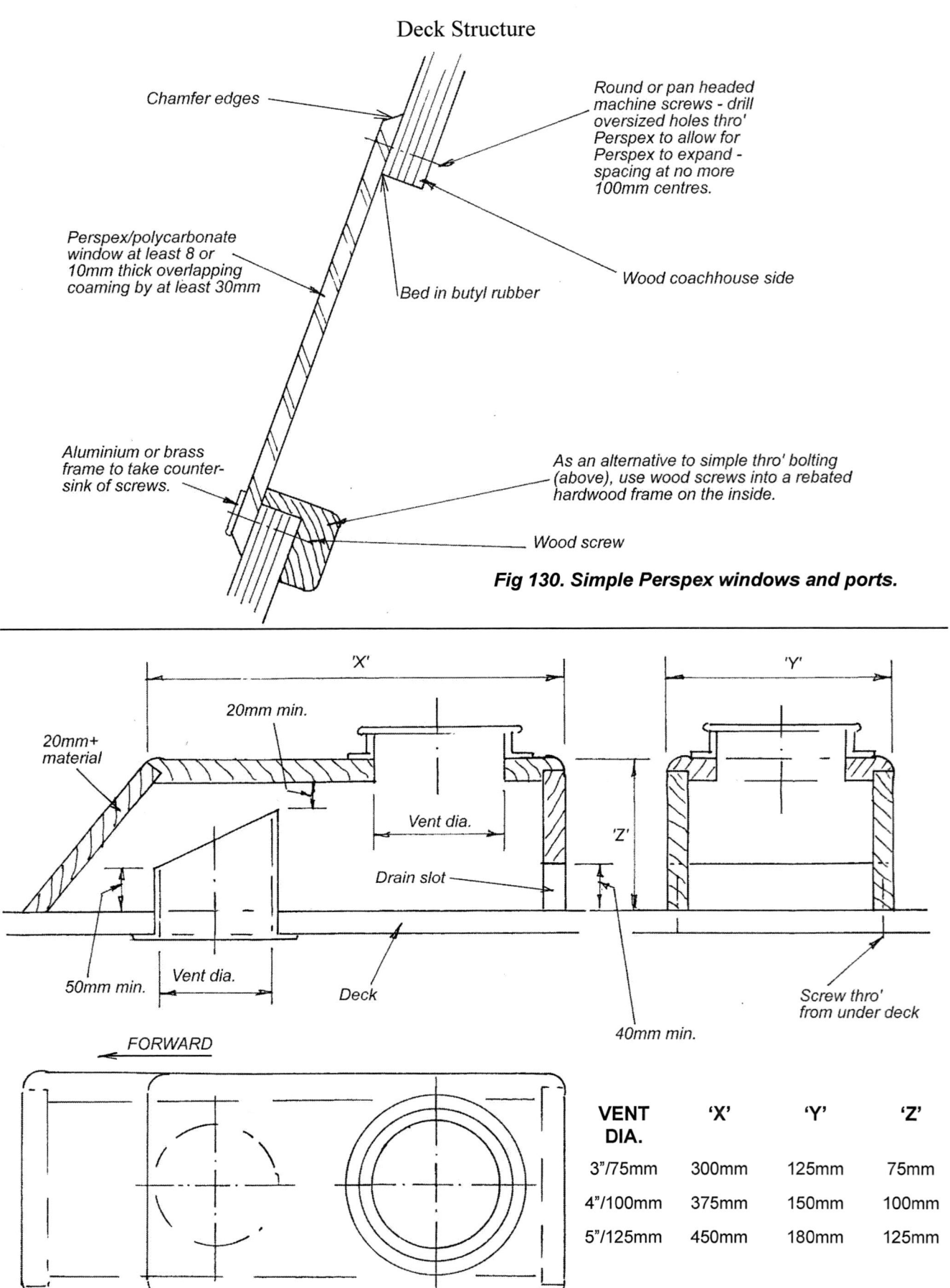

Chamfer edges

Round or pan headed machine screws - drill oversized holes thro' Perspex to allow for Perspex to expand - spacing at no more 100mm centres.

Perspex/polycarbonate window at least 8 or 10mm thick overlapping coaming by at least 30mm

Bed in butyl rubber

Wood coachhouse side

Aluminium or brass frame to take counter-sink of screws.

As an alternative to simple thro' bolting (above), use wood screws into a rebated hardwood frame on the inside.

Wood screw

Fig 130. Simple Perspex windows and ports.

'X'   'Y'

20mm min.

20mm+ material

Vent dia.

'Z'

Drain slot

50mm min.   Vent dia.

Deck

40mm min.

Screw thro' from under deck

FORWARD

VENT DIA.	'X'	'Y'	'Z'
3"/75mm	300mm	125mm	75mm
4"/100mm	375mm	150mm	100mm
5"/125mm	450mm	180mm	125mm

Fig 131. The Dorade Deck Vent.

Chapter 9

PAINTING & FINISHING

There are basically three broad paint systems that can be used to finish a boat :-

- 'Conventional' – usually single-pot paints and varnishes.
- 'High Performance' systems – often 2-pot and polyurethane based.
- Epoxy coating and sheathing which is then paint or varnish finished.

Which one you choose will come down to how much you are prepared to spend and where the boat is to be used. A general purpose workboat, constantly being scrapped on trailers or on the beach, will certainly benefit from a tough high performance paint or varnish, but the finish will quickly be ruined and so the question has to be asked, whether it is worth using a more expensive system under these circumstances.

We are dealing here with larger plywood boats and if you have invested considerably in the cost of the materials, and more so, in the construction time, it is silly not to compliment your boat with a well applied high quality finish.

High Performance systems do need more care taken in their application in terms of the humidity and temperature of the work space but, under normal use, they will keep their gloss longer and last a greater amount of time and protect the boat better, than conventional systems.

Epoxy coated and glass sheathed boats do need to be painted or varnished – if varnished, the varnish should have an ultra-violet filter in it as epoxy exposed to sunlight, will degrade over time.

Whichever system you choose, make sure you follow the manufacturer's instructions to the letter – in particular, if the boat is epoxy coated or epoxy/glass sheathed, make sure that the epoxy is completely cured before applying any paint or varnish. The epoxy surface may feel cured, but it is that last 0.001% of cure which, no matter how ideal the conditions, takes one or two weeks to complete. If the cure is not complete, problems will occur for subsequent coatings – either by throwing the paint/varnish off, or by not allowing the paint/varnish to cure at all. Be warned, paint not curing over an epoxy coated surface is a common problem – be patient!

No matter what system you use, the surfaces to be painted or varnished have to be prepared first and yes, it is worth repeating what every skilled painter says, *"in order to get a good finish, preparation is 75% of the battle"* – take you time!

Here is a typical preparation and painting sequence :-

• Search the surfaces to be painted for holes, gaps etc and fill – I use thickened epoxy.
• Once the filler has fully cured, carefully sand down and also search for any other bumps in the surface that need sanding down too – 80 to 100 grit sandpaper is used here. Filling the holes for screw heads is rarely done in one fill and so refill these where necessary and sand again.
• Carefully sand the whole surface with 120 to 180 grit sandpaper finishing off 'with the grain'.
• Spring clean your whole workshop and the boat itself – be fastidious in searching out and removing all dust and scrap material. If you do this on a sunny day, you will see the amount of dust you have disturbed in the air

which will resettle onto the boat's surface – so clean again.
• On the day that painting starts (and on subsequent painting days) some builders will 'damp down' the building floor etc to prevent dust circulating up.
• Decide on your painting sequence – ie where are you going to paint first – do not paint yourself into a corner. I tend to start on the interior of the boat first and work my way out.
• If at all possible, do the important painting on dry warm days with little moisture in the air – certainly do not paint early in the morning when there will be dampness in the atmosphere and temperatures are going to rise.
• Paint the first coat of primer (this is often thinned). Use the 'Union Jack' method by using diagonal strokes to spread the paint and then horizontal strokes, finishing off with vertical strokes. Work quickly keeping the working edges 'wet'.
• This first coat is a 'tell-tale' or 'indicator' coat so, when dry, inspect the surface for blemishes and areas that did not show up before, as dips etc and refill and sand again.
• I usually use another coat of primer but go by the paint manufacturer's instructions.
• Sand between coats using 280 to 320 grit paper.
• At least 3 coats of undercoat should be used, sanding between coats – I use 'wet and dry' paper with water at this and subsequent stages.
• If you are working on the outside of the hull, you may need to use a different undercoat for the anti-fouling – if so, after the primer, mask off the waterline whilst you finish the topsides.
At least 2 if not 3 coats of top coat should be applied, again, sanding between coats.
Varnished surfaces use much the same sequence (without the filling) with at least 5

and probably 7 or more coats (Silvers used to varnish with up to 15 coats!). If you are varnishing Iroko or Teak which have their own natural oils, you need to degrease them first with acetone.

Epoxy coated surfaces often need to be 'keyed' first with a light sanding, before they are painted.

Masts and spars are often varnished but some now coat in one of the many quick to apply oil products which are worth looking at as they can cut down on maintenance.

A SELECTION OF FINISHED
SELWAY FISHER DESIGNS

Above—the original Rufus 17 motor boat by Mr. Aley with hull finished and cabin under construction.

Above is a Ptarmigan 17 by Mr. P. Phillips showing a nicely varnished ply cabin side against her white topsides and coach roof.

Although not a plywood design, the example below of a strip planked Felix launch (by Mr. R. Miflin) shows a nicely planned deck of mahogany planks separated by strips of contrasting coloured wood and set off with a mahogany coaming.

Cabins are altered to suit the conditions— above is a Power 1.2 with it's wheelhouse omitted for use in the Far East—by Malcolm Kirke.

Right is a Simplicity 24 by Peter McDonald before the rubbing strakes were fitted to the topsides—the white topsides make her look big for her length.